WHERE

in Italy

Edited by
Chris Gill

Consultant Editor
Dave Watts

Contents

Foreword

by Konrad Bartelski

Italy came rather late in my skiing development, after I had first learned to ski in Austria and then in Scotland. It was not until I was looking to make my debut in an international FIS race that I ventured to Italy, and to the small village of Caspoggio, about 60 miles north-east of Milan.

With all the drama running through my nervous head, I can't have absorbed much of the character and style of the authentically traditional, quiet village. Yet I still vividly remember its charm and personality, which perhaps conveys something of the power of Italian culture – something that any skier should experience.

Even now, decades on from that first experience, I am still surprised by the sparkling gems that can be found in the Italian mountains, if one is prepared to explore and travel to new destinations.

And that is what I now find most rewarding: using my skis to get around the mountains and see new geography and sample different cuisines – things that Italy and the Italians excel at.

This is why this new guide is such a valuable tool, as Chris Gill and Dave Watts have taken the time to put down their experiences, from a British perspective, of the facilities and the options that are available in the different vibrant corners of the skiing mountains of Italy.

Without a doubt there is nowhere else that one can experience such genuinely brilliant and yet good-value dishes and wines, developed through centuries of social and political changes – and, perhaps, small and delicate changes that can make for wonderful surprises as you move between the different valleys.

The combination of the geography and history generates the same kaleidoscope effect, from the the spectacular and dramatic Alps, to the very different subtleties and enchanting colours of the Dolomites.

The spirit of the Italians is infectious, and certainly to understand this country one needs to have returned a few times to some of the contrasting regions to really comprehend the Italian magic.

For someone relatively new to Italian skiing, this new guide will be invaluable, introducing you to the best of those sparkling gems. But, even if you are already a fan, the book will give you the clear, balanced picture of each resort that you need to be confident of choosing the right one to visit next.

Kondrad Bartelski
21 August 2019

Editor's note In December 1981, Konrad stunned the ski-racing world by coming second, 0.11 seconds behind the winner, in the Val Gardena World Cup downhill race. No other British man matched that in any World Cup discipline until 2017, when Dave Ryding came second in the Kitzbühel slalom event.

◀ the scene of Konrad's momentous race (although the Saslong course is hidden)

About this book

by the editor

If you're a skier, you probably know *Where to Ski and Snowboard* – the annual guide to all the resorts that matter to a British skier, published from 1994 to 2015.

Or maybe you don't. WTSS, edited by me and Dave Watts, set the standard for ski resort guides for those 20-odd years, seeing off various rival books including *The Good Skiing Guide*, which I started back in the 1980s while I was editor of *Holiday Which?* magazine. WTSS became widely recognised as the British skier's bible.

Based on the same foundations of thorough research, impartial evaluation, warts-and-all text and reader-friendly layout, the book you're reading is the third in a new series of smaller guides, each dealing with a single country. *Where to Ski in Austria* was published in 2017, *Where to Ski in France* in 2018. Switzerland will follow, if all goes to plan. Various ebook versions are in the pipeline, too.

These books are all-new: they have been written from scratch, and have a new structure – an improved one, I hope. As you might expect, this volume covers more resorts in Italy than WTSS did: some resorts that made only occasional appearances in WTSS are back (Bardonecchia, Bormio, Kronplatz, Madesimo, Pila) and some in the Dolomites are here for the first time.

You might expect this book to cover the resorts in more detail, too. Well, it does and it doesn't. Some of the detail that seemed necessary in 1994 (or even 2004) is now made largely redundant by comprehensive resort websites and feedback sites such as TripAdvisor. So, some of that detail (on hotels, for example) has gone.

On the other hand, a book covering a limited range of resorts has room for more detailed analysis of the skiing. In these new books, beginners get more attention, and the broad church of intermediate skiers is split: the needs of cautious 'true blue' skiers are considered separately from those of confident red-run skiers.

Much of the redundant detail that has disappeared was also quick to go out of date. With that detail removed, annual revision starts to look extravagant; so these new books will stay on sale for several years before they are revised.

Where to Ski and Snowboard started life as *Where to Ski*. The 'Snowboard' was added in year three, after Dave and I decided to get to grips with boarding, and sent ourselves off to Colorado to take a course strictly for grown-ups. 20 years on, ski resorts are still called ski resorts. So the 'Snowboard' has gone.

Dave Watts is acting as consultant editor to this series, which means he is making contributions to some chapters based on his resort visits, and bringing his vast experience to bear by reviewing others. But I carry the can: comments and contradictions to me, please – or compliments, if you like.

Creating this book has been hard work, but I've really enjoyed the process; I hope you enjoy reading the result, and find it helps you decide ... where to ski in Italy.

Chris Gill
Exeter, 30 September 2019
chris.g@wheretoski.co.uk

Italy – an introduction

By the editor

Italy lags way behind Austria and France in holiday sales to the UK market. This is not surprising; for a start, it has fewer resorts that justify international interest (which also explains why this book is a bit shorter than the companion volumes on Austria and France). And it must be admitted that, with the stunning exception of the Sella Ronda area in the Dolomites, Italy lacks the large interlinked piste/lift networks that we've become used to in France – and are getting used to in Austria. (More on this aspect later.)

But Italy has an awful lot going for it. Many of the resorts are blessed by fabulous scenery – the Dolomites in particular is an area where the mountains are incredibly dramatic. They now have lift networks and snowmaking systems that are about the best in the Alps, and they prepare and maintain their pistes to a very high standard. The restaurants are generally excellent, serving food and wine that is not only delicious but also very good value by Alpine standards (and hot chocolate the like of which you find nowhere else).

Persuasive prices

The matter of prices is worth emphasising. In the latter years of *Where to Ski and Snowboard* we laboured to produce price indices comparing each resort with the average of all eurozone resorts. All Italian resorts were below average except Cortina d'Ampezzo and Madonna di Campiglio, and over half got a green index of 90 (meaning prices were about 90% of the eurozone average). In Austria, only one in five resorts got a green index.

Those index figures took account of lift passes, ski hire and lessons, as well as food and drink. In the early years of our price survey we looked only at restaurant prices, and the results were even more striking.

Vox pop

It's difficult to generalise about the style of Italian resorts. They range from polished valley-bottom towns to functional high-altitude ski stations, with plenty of traditional rustic villages in between. They are ranged across the whole width of the Alps, from the Via Lattea and resorts of Valle d'Aosta in the west, both spreading over the border into France, to Cortina in the eastern Dolomites.

Where to start in making a choice? Well, the opening pages of the resort chapters are designed to give an easily digested overview, so with their help you should be able to draw up a short-list without too much trouble. But we thought you might also find it helpful to know where your neighbours go. Here, in order of popularity, are the resorts favoured by the customers of two major package holiday operators to Italy:

Crystal Ski Passo Tonale / Sauze d'Oulx / Cervinia / Sestriere / La Thuile

Inghams Cortina d'Ampezzo / Sauze d'Oulx / Selva / Cervinia / Champoluc

Ski Italy

Home to some of Europe's best skiing, scenery, sunshine and cuisine

FEATURING

18 resorts and 100+ hotels

Fantastic ski areas including The Dolomites, a UNESCO World Heritage site

Flights from 7 regional airports from December - April

Top Tip!

Free lift passes and child places + discounted ski hire and tuition in selected resorts.

Visit **inghams.co.uk/skiitaly**

Call **01483 938 416**

Clearly, Sauze d'Oulx and Cervinia are popular places. Those resorts apart, though, why the major differences? We're guessing it's mainly down to dedicated accommodation. Crystal has two hotels exclusive to the company in Passo Tonale, and Inghams has two in Cortina and four in Selva. Equally, these firms would not have these lodgings if they weren't able to fill them.

The only slight surprise to us is La Thuile, where we haven't noticed huge numbers of Brits. But it's a resort well worth considering, particularly if you're looking to escape French school holiday crowds.

Escaping the crowds

Many Italian resorts, especially those that are easily reached from the cities of Italy's northern plains, get most of their Italian business at weekends. There are lots of apartments in these resorts used as second homes, and the lights come on within on Friday nights. This is tied in with the fact that Italian schools don't have a half-term holiday – just two or three days off for Carnevale (pancake day).

There are various results of all this. The crowd-free Saturday changeover phenomenon that is so pronounced in most French resorts doesn't really happen. Sundays are busier than Saturdays, because of day-trippers, but the whole weekend can be pretty busy.

On the other hand, weekdays can be deliciously quiet. And, what's more, they can be deliciously quiet in February, when the slopes in France are rammed. This seems to be most noticeable in La Thuile, as mentioned above.

None of this applies in the Südtirol – the part of the Dolomites that German skiers visit in large numbers, staying Saturday to Saturday. Nor does it apply in Livigno, which is too remote to attract weekenders and gets a lot of its visitors via a one-way road tunnel, resulting in very quite Saturdays.

Give us your money

As devotees of *Where to Ski and Snowboard* will know, your editors are quietly insistent that lunch, like dinner (or like lunch on a summer holiday), should be taken in restaurants with table service. Only in desperate circumstances will we resort to a self-service place. And in Italy, desperation isn't enough. We need to be feeling faint through lack of nourishment.

Why? Because of the Italian self-service payment system. It's usual for the cash to be handed over before the food or drinks, at a separate cash desk. So you have to work out what you want, which may mean you must queue to inspect the goods at the food counter, then queue to do the deal at the cash desk, then queue again to get your grub. Forgot to order a side salad? Decide you like the look of the tiramisu? Off you go, back to the cash desk queue.

This system is insane. Our guess is it was devised to stop fraud – the cash is often taken by a dragon who obviously owns the place and wouldn't trust anyone else with her takings.

Fortunately, table service is easy to find.

Snow business

Most of the weather that hits the Alps comes from the west, roughly speaking, and quite a bit of it from points north of west. This means that Italian resorts, sitting to the east of the French Alps and south of the Swiss and Austrian Alps, sometimes miss out on snowfall that their neighbours enjoy.

When the weather comes more from the south, of course, Italian resorts do well, sometimes very well indeed. We've been in the Dolomites at times when most of the roads in and out were impassable, forcing us to use a very roundabout route to get back to Venice airport. And sometimes Mediterranean storms mean that the resorts in the maritime Alps, way down south of Turin, get the most snow of all.

The upside of Italy's erratic snow record is that Italian resorts got into snowmaking early, and understand how important it is to use it sensibly – that is, before a lack of natural snow becomes a problem. In the Dolomites, in particular, you can have a wonderful holiday cruising on beautifully prepared pistes even at time when there is essentially no natural snow.

Easy does it

One doesn't want to draw on stereotypes, but it does seem that Italians perhaps like to be flattered when skiing: piste classification in Italian resorts often tends to overstate difficulty. Cervinia, Monterosa and La Thuile are examples of resorts where there are many red runs that elsewhere might be classified blue. (The

Look after yourself

In these new guides I have tried to give direct guidance to specific groups of skiers about which resorts and even which runs will suit them. In particular, I have tried to help a group that we perhaps neglected slightly in the many editions of *Where to Ski and Snowboard*: the inexperienced, not entirely competent or confident, early intermediate skier.

Obviously, giving clear guidance of this kind is problematic. I don't know your individual abilities or how well equipped you are, or the conditions you'll meet; I can't guarantee that the judgements Dave and I have made are consistent from day to day, or year to year, however hard we try.

So I have to say that you should not plan your week, and still less your day, solely on the basis of what you read here. Treat this book as a starting point. If you haven't reached the stage where you can get down any intermediate slope (given time), you should be skiing with someone who knows the slopes and understands the conditions. This might mean an instructor.

At the other end of the scale, this book also spells out the opportunities in each resort for off-piste skiing – or freeriding, as it is now branded. Off-piste skiing is inherently dangerous; it requires specialised skills, equipment and – crucially – knowledge, some of it general and some of it very local. For most people, the only safe way to do it is with professional guidance.

pattern is not universal, however – there are one or two red runs in Selva, for example, that might be better classified black.)

This overstatement may lead confident red-run skiers to be disappointed by an area's lack of challenge, but the bigger problem it creates is that blue-run skiers who get used to cruising on easy reds can get a bit of a shock when they encounter a genuine red piste – and such things of course do exist.

The high standard of piste maintenance referred to earlier reinforces the impression of flattering slopes – pretty well all pistes are groomed daily and thoroughly, black runs included. Moguls can form on groomed pistes, of course, but they are rarely left to mature.

Off-piste, anyone?

In some Italian resorts – mainly in the Dolomites, in our experience – you will occasionally see signs warning you that off-piste skiing is prohibited, and if you read around the subject you'll find different sources telling you that it's prohibited near lifts and pistes, or outside defined routes, or without a guide, or without a transceiver, or in any circumstances at all.

Requiring off-piste skiers to have transceivers makes obvious sense, but restricting off-piste skiing on the basis that it endangers those using lifts and pistes makes much less sense. Yes, off-piste skiers can trigger an avalanche, but only on a slope that is waiting to avalanche. If there is such a slope above a lift or piste, the solution is to make it safe, before some other trigger releases the slide.

In other areas, it's not so much permitted as encouraged – in the Monterosa area, for example, the top cable car serves only the off-piste terrain for which the area is famous, and one route is marked on the piste map (now without explanation).

A similar situation is found in Madesimo, on the famous Canalone run: it is marked on the map but the lift company insists it is absolutely off-piste. The bizarre thing here is that the run is – or as least has been – also marked on the mountain (for the benefit of staff, says the lift company). Marked itineraries need to be opened and closed according to avalanche risk.

Even marking an off-piste route on a resort's piste map is inviting tragedy. Courmayeur has several routes marked on its map, and in February 2019 two British skiers died in an avalanche while skiing one of them. At the coroner's inquest, family members are reported to have expressed the view that the run was not a proper off-piste run but was a marked itinerary, with the implication that it should have been safe.

The piste map calls the route *fuori pista* in Italian, and we're pretty clear that means off-piste. In English, though, the map uses the term 'freeride area' rather than 'off-piste', which is perhaps less clear. Clarity is needed in such things, and for that we needed fewer terms used consistently, not more. Most of us know what 'off-piste' means, but 'freeride' is used in various ways.

Zermatt, in Switzerland but linked to Cervinia in Italy, long ago redefined many of its best black pistes as unprepared itineraries, calling them 'itineraires ski runs'. It now calls them 'freeriding pistes', and its website explains they are 'non-prepared pistes, which have otherwise been made safe from Alpine dangers'. The lift company confirms that they are, in effect, just ungroomed pistes. Meanwhile, the Cervinia version of the map covering the shared area calls them 'Fuoripista - Abfahrtsroute - Freeride'.

So both resorts employ the word 'freeride', but visitors to Zermatt are being told these runs are ungroomed black pistes, while visitors to Cervinia popping over to ski them are doing so with full avalanche gear on their backs. This lack of consistency is mad and unnecessary, and helps to create dangerous confusion.

The linking run fiasco

There's something strange going on in Italian resorts in the minor but not necessarily unimportant matter of link runs – runs that cross the mountainside, often but not always narrow cat-tracks, to link one part of the mountain to another. Incredibly, some resorts have withdrawn piste status from these runs.

We encountered the problem first in Cortina, in 2019: short runs at mid-mountain marked on the piste map in green, without explanation. We set off to investigate, expecting to find beginner slopes of some sort, like the green runs common in France. On the mountain, we could see no green signs or poles, no relevant piste-side maps or notices. We didn't find notably gentle slopes, either.

On return home, we dug out an old piste map which did have an explanation of the green runs: '*percorsi non controllati* / not controlled ski tracks'. Unable to believe that there might be pistes on the mountain that were not patrolled, we grilled the tourist office; they confirmed that these runs are not patrolled (and that they'll be restoring the explanation to next season's piste map). All of which is ridiculous. Are they serious about not patrolling? How could they be, when there is nothing on the mountain to inform skiers of the runs' status?

Even if the runs are patrolled, there will still be the problem of skiers not finding the explanation, making the natural assumption that these green runs are French-style very easy pistes, and getting a nasty shock when they find they are no such thing. One reader reported exactly this in 2019.

In Bormio we found a related but different situation. Here, half a dozen of the 18 named pistes were described on the map as '*skiwegs*', meaning that they are cat-track links across the hill. Most were classified red, which seemed odd. When we came to ski some of them, we found the sign shown in our photo. Incredibly, here too the tourist office confirmed the situation: these groomed red runs are not formally pistes – not part of the secured ski area. Strictly speaking you shouldn't ski them without avalanche kit.

We cannot believe that the green runs in Cortina are not patrolled, or that the red *skiwegs* in Bormio are at risk of avalanche. Our guess is that the explanation is the Italian talent for bureaucracy – that these runs have fallen foul of some half-baked regulation which means they can't be advertised as pistes. So the bureaucrats can tick the appropriate box, and we skiers are left trying to figure out what on earth is going on.

Size matters here, too

If you are among the many British skiers for whom a properly enjoyable ski holiday requires a big ski area, skiing at least some new terrain every day, your Italian options are much more limited than your French ones.

Italy does have one of the biggest areas of all: the Sella Ronda in the Dolomites, with something like 400km of pistes, comes fourth in the global rankings after the French Trois Vallées and Paradiski, and the Franco-Swiss Portes du Soleil, and well ahead of Austria's Arlberg and Saalbach areas. It is the one Italian area to get our ✳✳✳✳✳ rating for size.

On the next rung down, Italy is again rather put in the shade by France. There are five French areas in our ✳✳✳✳ size category, and only two Italian ones – or, to be more accurate, two international ones with an Italian component. And neither of the latter works entirely smoothly.

The Matterhorn area linking Cervinia with Swiss Zermatt sprawls over such distances that it is difficult to make the most of the Swiss side from Cervinia. It also relies on a very high, exposed link, but that will work better now that improved lifts make it less prone to closure by high winds. The Via Lattea area linking Sauze d'Oulx and Sestriere with Claviere and French Montgenèvre has the inverse problem – a very low link with no pistes to the valley bottom and slow old chair-lifts on the Claviere side of the valley. (Be aware also that in 2019 some key linking pistes were closed following a tragic accident – read the Via Lattea chapter.)

The core of Italian skiing is the wide choice of smaller resorts that get ✳✳✳ or ✳✳ size ratings. There are nine such resorts in these pages. Some skiers are happy spending a week in areas of this size, others not. But it's worth noting that practically all have lift pass sharing arrangements with other resorts within striking distance by car, bus or train.

We've also found room in these pages to give chapters to three resorts with ✳ size ratings, meaning less than 50km of pistes. Courmayeur and Pila are in the

Valle d'Aosta and are easily combined with one another or with other resorts in the valley – there is limited lift pass sharing, and a valley pass that allows you to ski wherever you like. Madesimo, in a remote valley near the Swiss border, is not easily combined with anywhere. But it has attractions; prices are low, even by Italian standards – most of the hotels are 2-stars, and a 6-day pass cost under €200 in 2019. Oh, and it has the best snowmobiling we've experienced.

We've also covered four small ski areas that don't see many British visitors, in the penultimate chapter of the book, Southern Dolomites.

But how long is a piece of piste?

There is still immense confusion in the ski resort business over piste extent. Many resorts (and practically all Italian resorts) like to inflate their assets by taking the length of their pistes and applying a multiplier, on the basis that skiers don't go straight down the runs – they make turns, and therefore travel further. Faithful readers of *Where to Ski and Snowboard* will be aware of the campaign we ran for years about this nonsense, focusing particularly on the Italian resorts of Courmayeur and Monterosa.

This mess has been illuminated by the work of a dedicated German consultant, Christoph Schrahe, who has digitally measured the runs of the world's top 100 resorts (and more). He has published his findings, and you'll find many references to them in these pages. Naturally, he uses no multiplier, and in almost all cases he found that resort figures overstate the extent of the resort's pistes, often by very considerable amounts.

Christoph has had some success in persuading resorts to publish sensible piste km figures; the Franco-Italian Espace San Bernardo is one area that has had its extent verified by him. But he now seems to have gone off in a different direction, promoting a new measure of ski resort size based on an elaborate calculation involving ten weighted factors – including piste km but also overall vertical, skiable area and so on. We wish Christoph well in his new venture, but we'll be sticking to piste km – and so, we suspect, will practically everyone else.

Molto grazie

In compiling this book we have been able to draw on a healthy bunch of reports from readers about their holidays in Italy over the last couple of seasons. If you were among those readers and your report was in any way useful, you should now be reading the free copy we have sent as a token of our thanks. Your help is much appreciated.

If, as we hope, this book is followed by one on Switzerland, we'll be inviting reports on holidays there too. There will be information on our website wheretoskiandsnowboard.com in due course.

If you want to be kept abreast of our publishing plans, or kept informed about ski resort developments, sign up for our mailing list on that site.

Practicalities: getting there

Italian resorts vary hugely in how easily accessible they are by car, from valley bottom Courmayeur, just the far side of the Mont Blanc tunnel (570 miles from Calais), to high and remote Livigno and the distant Dolomites (Arabba is 750 miles from Calais).

The resorts west of Turin are easily reached via the Fréjus road tunnel, which delivers you directly to Bardonecchia. The Valle d'Aosta resorts are most obviously reached via the Mont Blanc tunnel, which ends close to Courmayeur. Note that these tunnels are not cheap – about €60 return. Bear in mind that some resorts have long access roads up from the valley.

The Alta Valtellina resorts – Livigno and Bormio – are best reached by tunnel from Switzerland, but resorts further east – all the Dolomites resorts – are best reached via the Brenner pass from Innsbruck, which is a motorway and pretty well guaranteed to be kept open.

Air travellers need to be aware of transfer times, which range from the negligible to the considerable. There's a wide choice of arrival airports, shown on the maps inside the covers of the book. The preferable choices are mainly obvious.

For Cortina, Venice is obviously quite convenient, and offers the tempting possibility of a night or two in Venice before flying home. Be wary of Treviso airport, which is prone to fog, doesn't have state-of-the-art landing systems, and is a pretty miserable place in which to be trapped. For Dolomites resorts further west, Innsbruck in Austria will often be the best bet – over the Brenner pass.

Innsbruck is also the best airport for Livigno, and worth considering for Bormio. Bergamo and Milan Linate are viable for resorts in the eastern half of the Alps, too.

For the Aosta valley resorts Turin looks a likely choice, but it doesn't have a great range of flights. You may find Geneva and the Mont Blanc tunnel make more sense than flying to Milan.

In general, rail travel to Italian resorts is hard work. But the Fréjus rail tunnel will deliver you directly to Bardonecchia, and from Oulx station nearby you can quickly get up to Sauze d'Oulx.

If you are planning to fly or train and then hire a car, take care. Italian hire cars are not routinely equipped with winter tyres, which are essential unless you are staying at low altitude. Unless you can find a hire company that confirms that you are getting winter tyres, it's better to hire in Switzerland or Austria. Diesel cars hired at low airports are also not routinely filled with winter fuel, so if you are going high you theoretically need to add an anti-waxing substance (or fill up as soon as you get to your resort).

Alta Valtellina

Bormio / Cima Piazzi / Santa Caterina / Livigno

A multi-resort pass makes for an interesting week

The name of this region probably isn't familiar, but the major resorts are quite well known, and are set to get more so — the 2026 Olympic Winter Games have been awarded to Milan-Cortina, but the men's Alpine races will be held in Bormio, and snowboard and freestyle events in Livigno.

The resort best known in Britain is Livigno. It is very unusual in being an attractive, traditional mountain village at high altitude (over 1800m) with modest prices, thanks to its duty-free status. The altitude doesn't mean huge snowfall — this is quite a dry part of the Alps. But it does mean any precipitation is likely to be crystalline.

But we're giving pride of place to Bormio — a captivating historic town, with skiing (if you take in adjacent Cima Piazzi and nearby Santa Caterina) that's at least as interesting as that of Livigno. Twenty years ago, a dozen tour operators were taking British skiers here. Is it due for a revival?

Certainly access to Bormio, a problem in the past, these days is bearable — allow 3hr from Milan or Bergamo airports. Via Bormio, Livigno takes another hour, and involves the 2300m Passo di Foscagno, which can of course be affected by snowfall — so the favoured route is from Innsbruck in Austria, via Switzerland. This also takes about 3hr, provided you don't hit a queue for the single-track Munt la Schera tunnel, which can arise in high season; on Saturdays it is largely given over to inbound traffic, which helps.

The Bormio lift pass also covers Cima Piazzi and S Caterina, and we deal with these areas under Bormio. The Alta Valtellina lift pass also covers Livigno. The nearest of its lifts is only about 45 minutes away at Trepalle, and it's well worth making the trip a time or two during your week.

North-west of Bormio, 8km away as the eagle flies, is the glacier skiing area of Passo Stelvio, claimed to be the biggest summer skiing area in the Alps. It's open only from May through October, so it is not covered here.

Bormio

Bormio is a one-off – a historic Alpine crossroads with a charming centre of largely car-free cobbled streets and ancient monuments. It's animated in the evening, as much by local families as by visiting skiers looking to party.

Its local mountain is unusual, too – although very tall, it is very slim; at its widest, the lift system is no more than 1km across. More importantly, it is very much a red-run mountain, with little to offer our true blue skier. The same is true of the other hills in the area, Cima Piazzi and S Caterina.

Bormio may not feel like a ski resort, but it is a major race venue, regularly running World Cup downhills and the English Alpine Championships, twice hosting the Alpine World Championships and now set to hold the men's Olympic Alpine races.

The mountains in brief

Size The three local hills don't add up to a lot, but then there's also Livigno

Slopes Big verticals on mainly open slopes at Bormio

Snow Not known for dumps, but altitude, orientation and snow-guns all help

System, Lift Ageing, but it copes; lots of slow lifts at C Piazzi and S Caterina

Sustenance Hardly a highlight, but some decent spots

For beginners Nursery slopes OK, but progression is tricky, because ...

For true blue skiers Look elsewhere (Livigno's better, though not ideal)

For the confident These mountains could have been made for you

For experts Few piste challenges, but worthwhile off-piste areas

Fancy stuff Bormio now has a full set of terrain features

Bormio – the resort in brief

Convenience You can stay near a lift; but you'll want to take some buses

Lodgings A good range of hotels, including some rather special ones

Bars and restaurants Bormio's a lively town, with lots of attractive spots

Off the slopes More spas than you can sensibly use, and good skating

For families Bormio's not an obvious candidate for a family trip

Pass notes	Key facts		Key ratings	
The Bormio pass covers Cima Piazzi and Santa Caterina as well, but the six-day Alta Valtellina pass also covering Livigno (and linking buses) cost only €34 more in 2019. Beginners need passes to reach the main mid-mountain nursery slopes. Day and half-day passes for each mountain are available.	Altitude	1200m	Size	**
	Range	1200–3018m	Snow	***
	Slopes (see text)	63km	Fast lifts	***
	Where to stay, ideally		Mountain rest's	***
	Near the Bormio gondola.		Beginner	**
			True blue	*
	Websites		Confident	****
	bormio.eu		Expert	***
	bormioski.eu		Convenience	***
	bormioskipass.eu		Families	**
			Village charm	****

The mountains in detail

A powerful gondola takes you to the heart of the Bormio skiing at Bormio 2000, where there is an array of restaurants, several short lifts and two long ones — the fast Cimino quad chair, accessing most of the upper mountain, and a mid-sized cable car rising over 1000m to the top, Cima Bianca. On the upper mountain is a complex web of mainly red runs extending to Ciuk, 300m lower than Bormio 2000.

A 15-minute bus ride away at Isolaccia, in Valdidentro on the road to Livigno, is a gondola station accessing a small area of slopes linked at altitude with slopes above a second (slow) access lift at Le Motte. Traditionally called San Colombano, it's being rebranded as Cima Piazzi.

A 30-minute ride in the opposite direction is S Caterina, where a two-stage gondola from a base well outside the village serves black runs on the upper slopes and red runs lower down, where it is supplemented by slow lifts. From the village, a slow chair-lift gives access. The gondola goes on over the ridge and down a little way to Sunny Valley Lodge and a long chair-lift to the area high point at 2880m, serving further red pistes. You can ride the gondola back to the front side, or take a roundabout red piste.

Note that these bus services are not frequent; you'll need timetables, or the willingness to sit in a bar waiting for the last bus home.

Size

Bormio claims 50km of pistes, Cima Piazzi 25km and S Caterina a further 35km, for a claimed grand total of 110km; but having skied the hills, we view all these figures with scepticism. The S Caterina piste map states lengths for each piste, and a bit of digital measurement confirms that they are about right; these lengths total 20km, which seems much nearer the mark. Applying the same fact:fantasy ratio to the Bormio and Cima Piazzi figures gives a plausible real total of 63km for the three areas combined – which means a ✱✱ size rating.

Slopes

The upper mountain above Bormio 2000, where you spend most of your time, is mostly open, but the lowest quarter of it is wooded. It's a classic red-run hill, with few runs that are easier or much steeper.

The mountain offers a total vertical of almost 1800m – advertised as Italy's biggest – and over 1000m from the top to the main lift base at Bormio 2000. Top to bottom it's about 7km, although you can make it longer if you set about it.

Cima Piazzi offers 1000m vertical of wooded runs, plus an open area beyond that. At S Caterina there's a pretty clear division between the woodland red runs served by the access lifts and the open upper slopes. From the ridge to the base is 1000m vertical, which you can do entirely on red pistes – around 4km.

Half a dozen of Bormio's 18 named pistes are classified as 'skiwegs', meaning that they are cat-track links across the hill. But most are classified red and are signed as 'ski itineraries', used at your own risk. Incredibly, the tourist office confirms the situation – these prepared runs are not part of the secured ski area. Astonishing.

Snow

This is not a notably snowy area, but much of the Bormio skiing is above 2000m and it faces roughly north. With 190 fixed snow-guns and 50 mobile ones, snowmaking is now claimed to cover 80% of the pistes. So you can be fairly confident of good snow, at least on the upper part of the main mountain. Cima Piazzi is lower, but still generally shady (one arm faces more like east than north, which is nearly as good). At 1730m, S Caterina is appreciably higher than the other resorts. The front of the hill is shady, the back sunny but high – all above 2500m. Overall, a good bet.

System, Lift

The Bormio system is hardly state-of-the-art – even the three long, fast chair-lifts that form the backbone of the network are quads over 15 years old – but it seems to cope with demand. The two slow chairs are quite short (under 1km).

Cima Piazzi is in a bit of a time warp, with half the area served entirely by slow chair-lifts, the other half largely by drags. We and readers have found the slopes here very quiet, even in high season.

S Caterina's system is designed for day-visitor invasions, with a gondola starting outside the village beside multi-storey parking. The long quad chair on the back of the hill is fast, but serves limited vertical. The other lifts are slow.

Sustenance

Heaven 3000, at the top of Bormio, wins no awards for ambience but can't be beaten for views – and the food gets good reports. There are several places at Bormio 2000 and Ciuk. But our pick would be the Rododendri a bit higher up at La Rocca (marked on the piste map) – excellent food and service in a comfortable setting. The next-door restaurant – actually called La Rocca – gets good reports, too.

At Cima Piazzi there's a decent choice of places. At S Caterina there's a handful of places on the front side, mostly around the base of the drag-lifts at mid-mountain; Sci 2000 gets generally good reports. But the key place is on the back side of the hill: the log-built Sunny Valley lodge, at the gondola station – a great spot, with interesting food.

More on the slopes

For beginners

There is a carpet-lift next to the Bormio gondola station and another up at Ciuk, but most of the beginner slopes are further up at Bormio 2000 – two carpets are complemented by three longer drags.

But progression to longer runs isn't easy – read the following section.

For true blue skiers

Although there are runs that are towards the easier end of the red spectrum, there is not a lot for true blue skiers to do at Bormio. At Bormio 2000 the 600m Nevada Ovest drag serves two blue runs, though one of them feeds into an easy red. For those prepared to take a red 'skiweg' the Pian dei Larici chair-lift

A great view of the main Bormio mountain from the top of the Cima Piazzi lift system

accesses a longer blue. There is a blue run from Ciuk to the gondola base, but no easy way to get to it (except by road).

Over at Cima Piazzi, the slow quad chair-lift from Le Motte serves a blue winding through the woods. And at mid-mountain above Isolaccia there is a short blue run; there is also higher blue skiing, but access involves skiing red runs.

At S Caterina the village access chair-lift takes you to blue runs down either side of a 565m drag-lift (which bizarrely was not working when we visited in 2019). The run back to the village is red, and not the easiest; we're told you can ride the chair down, to avoid it.

This is all far from satisfactory, and blue-run skiers shouldn't be tempted to come here. Many resorts make much more sense for skiers lacking confidence – Livigno among them.

For confident intermediates

Putting aside the limited size of the area, Bormio's mountain is excellent for confident intermediates, with varied, long and satisfying runs. Roughly speaking, there are two runs from the top to Bormio 2000 – Bimbi al Sole outside the lift system on skier's left and Stella Alpina down the middle. Then there's Sant Ambrogio down the long chair-lift on skier's right of the lift system. We particularly like Bimbi al Sole, which seems less busy than the others.

And then there is Bormio's claim to fame – the Stelvio downhill race course. One of the most challenging courses on the World Cup circuit, it starts just above La Rocca and drops more than 1000m over a distance of about 3250m to the gondola base.

Several of these elements are stitched together to form the course of Peak to Creek, a top-to-bottom, all-comers fun race that takes place in January, attracting several hundred entrants. To add to the fun, you start in pairs.

Cima Piazzi is well worth a visit, particularly in good conditions when you might enjoy laps on the one fast lift, the 650m vertical gondola from Isolaccia.

Mostly S Caterina offers genuine red-run skiing, steeper on the shady front than on the sunny back of the hill, and generally good snow. The fast chair on the back of the hill seems an obvious target, but it has a vertical of only 340m,

and the skiing is not very challenging. The roundabout red to return to the front side is good fun.

For experts

Bormio has one black piste, the 400m-vertical Betulle. It has a serious pitch shortly after the start, and a less steep proper black stretch two-thirds of the way down, but mostly is of tough red gradient.

On the open upper mountain there are off-piste opportunities near the pistes, but the main attraction is the broad bowl to skier's left of the piste system, Vallone. Hiking up the ridge towards M Vallecetta opens up more exciting (and dangerous) terrain. There are also routes on the south side of the ridge, ending at the Valfurva road for a bus home.

You can also descend to skier's right of the lift system into the trees, which start as glades but get much tighter.

At Cima Piazzi the Dosso le Pone drag at the top is the place to head. There is a glorious area of easy off-piste next to the lift, but also on the back of the hill there are some long descents over open snowfields and on to forest trails to return to Isolaccia. A bit of hiking towards Pizzo Borron opens up more serious routes.

The black runs on the upper front face at S Caterina go over some steep, rocky terrain at the top; they mainly cut across it, but there are some steep pitches before the runs mellow around mid-mountain. The one on skier's left is the Deborah Compagnoni World Cup downhill race course, named after the famously successful local racer. There is plenty of opportunity to get off-piste on both faces of the mountain. On the front, there are routes down into the piste network from the top station of the gondola, but the more interesting routes are reached via the fast chair-lift on the back of the hill, followed by a bit of walking along the ridge. Skinning up to M Sobretta opens up some superb routes down into the valley beneath Cima Bianca, again ending at the Valfurva road for a bus home.

Fancy stuff

Bormio now offers a regular snow park with kickers etc served by the 850m Rocca Est T-bar, plus several less serious options – a funslope and the Familypark above Bormio 2000, and another funslope higher up.

Bormio – the resort

It's a resort of two halves, separated by the river Frodolfo. Around the gondola station is a modern suburb of chalet-style hotels. A pedestrian bridge takes you across the river and valley road to the charming old town, a maze of narrow cobbled streets set on a gentle slope; its main focus is Piazza Cavour, with an ornate church, a bell tower of medieval origin and a 14thC but reconstructed town 'forum' (the Kuerc). It's not all quite so lovely, of course: the town spreads widely into more modern fringes, with the Milan–Livigno/Stelvio road passing through the western part.

Convenience

You can keep your plodding to the minimum by staying near the gondola station, paying the bearable price of a 600m walk to the via Roma in the heart of the old town to sample the evening atmosphere. Once upon a time there was a second access lift 300m east of the gondola. Its removal means that lodgings towards the east end of the lift base area are no more convenient than some of the hotels in or around the old town.

If tempted by hotels further afield, you can use buses (on several colour-coded lines) to get to and from the lift; the better hotels also run shuttle-buses.

Lodgings

There are abundant 4-star and 3-star hotels. The 3-star hotel Alù gets good reports and is well placed for the gondola, although the Nevada is in pole position. In a good compromise location is the 4-star Baita dei Pini, on the town side of the linking road bridge.

Out of the ordinary

A couple of miles from the lifts, up the road towards Passo Stelvio, is the charming 4-star hotel Bagni Vecchi, complete with Roman baths (they say) and great views. A more compelling option for the keen skier is the excellent 3-star hotel Vallechiara, on the piste up at Ciuk.

Bormio Terme, the thermal spa that's set in the old town, with the ski hill visible across the valley

Bars and restaurants

La Rocca is popular for a late afternoon glass or two, and there are bars around the lift base that can be quite lively – Be White is right at the lift station. As you walk over the bridge to the old town, glance down to your left and you'll spot Oliver – a big American-style sports bar doing good burgers and steaks. Don't count on getting them to show Six Nations matches, though. Not far away in via Fiera is the more atmospheric Clem Pub, with complimentary antipasti.

Keep heading north and you'll find yourself in via Roma, with a whole string of attractive places. For a serious meal with serious wine, take a look at Enoteca Guanella. There are countless other options in the old town. For more down-to-earth local dishes in a very traditional setting, head back to the gondola area and to La Rasiga (The Sawmill) in the old village at the far eastern end.

Off the slopes

Palaghiaccio ('ice palace') houses a big ice rink used for hockey and short-track racing as well as for routine skating. There's also a curling rink, and a tennis hall. The Bormio Terme thermal spa has all sorts of pools, including a 25m sports pool, a seriously warm outdoor pool and pools for kids. The thermal spas of Bagni Nuovi and Bagni Vecchi, slightly out of town, are also open to the public although attached to hotels, and a ski+spa pass covering these is available. There is cross-country skiing at the foot of all three mountains – appreciably more at Isolaccia and S Caterina than at Bormio. Near Isolaccia is a well-known dog-sledding centre.

For families

Bormio has considerable appeal for families, provided you are not expecting your infants to find lots of English-speaking chums in the ski kindergarten. The child-oriented fun features on the hill are now quite extensive, and there is a snow garden at the gondola station (not free, sadly). The ice rink and spa pools are excellent.

Choice of lodgings is important: to make late-afternoon sledging as easy as possible, you might want to consider a hotel up on the slopes – we've tipped one in 'Lodgings', but there are others.

The other resorts

Isolaccia 1345m

Isolaccia is a quiet valley village rather than a ski resort, although the Cima Piazzi gondola is on the outskirts. It's pleasant and spacious, with a handsome church at its heart.

You might think of staying here to be strategically positioned between Bormio (20 minutes away) and Livigno (about 25 minutes to the nearest lifts at Trepalle). There are several hotels; the 3-star Cima Piazzi is well placed between the centre and the gondola. There's a natural ice rink. For beginners there are carpet-lifts at mid-mountain, with a drag-lift nearby serving an easy blue run.

Santa Caterina 1730m

Santa Caterina could scarcely be more different from Bormio – a quiet, traditional although rather plain village tucked away in the high Valfurva – a dead end in winter when the Passo Gavia to Ponte di Legno is closed.

Whereas we can see the case for staying in Isolaccia, it's difficult to see the case for staying here – in practical terms, half an hour from the skiing of Bormio but much more from the skiing of Livigno.

For lodgings you have three basic options. Stay in the unremarkable village (perhaps in the central, riverside Sport or in Deborah Compagnoni's Baita Fiorita – both 3-star), and put up with slow mountain access. Or stay near the gondola station (perhaps in the next-door Genzianella, or up the hill a bit in the simple, piste-side Baita Sciatori). Or splurge on splendid isolation in one of 11 lovely suites in the smart wood-built Sunny Valley lodge, over the ridge and reached by the gondola. This last may be one good reason to stay in S Caterina.

There's a nursery slope with a 60m carpet-lift at the village lift base (not free, surprisingly). There's also a free carpet lift at Sunny Valley lodge on the back of the hill, presumably for the convenience of people staying there – it makes little sense for anyone else.

There is an outdoor ice rink, with floodlights. Cross-country skiers are well catered for, with some serious trails for racers as well as easier tourist trails. A walks leaflet can be downloaded.

Livigno 1815m

Livigno is another unusual resort – built entirely in low-rise chalet style but high and cold, with a good chance of excellent snow. Not surprisingly, some people love the place. We've never quite fallen for it: the skiing (on either side of the village, linked by buses) is mostly on rather featureless open slopes, and the resort, although pleasantly rustic, is the ultimate ribbon development – 5km long, with the main lift bases 2.5km apart.

The mountains

It's a simple arrangement. West of the long village, lifts go up from the north end to the mountain ridge via Costaccia and from the south end to higher Carosello; these lifts are linked at altitude. Across the valley, similarly, lifts from opposite ends of the suburb of Teola go up to Mottolino and to higher Monte della Neve, again linked at altitude. Each ridge has a bit of skiing on the back side – on Mottolino, a lift at Trepalle offers the most immediate way in to the system for visitors from Bormio. Frequent shuttle-buses now link the lift bases of the two ski areas at both north and sound ends, in addition to the regular ski-bus services.

Size When added together, Livigno's two ski areas are claimed to amount to 115km of pistes. Christoph Schrahe's work (read the introduction to the book) has shown that this overstates the reality by about a third, so in fact it's not a big area – it rates two stars on our five-star scale. In purely factual terms, the resort offers comfortably more skiing than the combined total of Bormio and its two closer neighbours. But bear in mind what we say under 'For the confident' about the lack of variety here.

Slopes The mountains offer a good range of intermediate gradients, mainly on open slopes; on the Mottolino side in particular there is a fair area of forest, but not many runs cut through it – probably because of the difficulties presented by

Mottolino from Carosello – extensive trees, but not many pistes within them; note the veeeery long village

the road to Bormio, which snakes up across the hillside.

The resort map marks the top of the Carosello gondola as 'Carosello 3000 2797m' but the actual altitude is 2749m. Monte della Neve, similarly, is marked as 2785m; that is indeed the height of the mountain, but the lift station is at 2708m. Even so, both sectors offer a respectable descent of about 900m vertical to the village. More often you'll be skiing runs on chair-lifts with verticals about half that. On each mountain there are runs to the valley of up to 5 or 6km in length.

The pistes are neither named nor numbered on the mountain map.

Snow Like nearby St Moritz, Livigno has a better sunshine record than snowfall record, but the climate is cold, so snowfall starts early in the season and whatever falls persists well – and there is extensive snowmaking. The back of Carosello gets the afternoon sun, but Mottolino's slopes face well north of west, so aren't affected so much. We've generally found good conditions here, as have most readers.

System, Lift The lift system is modern and efficient, dominated by gondolas and fast chair-lifts. None of the four slow chairs is in a key position, although a replacement for the Blesaccia I triple in the middle of the Carosello slopes would be welcome. Queues are rare; delays can arise at the gondolas at peak times.

Sustenance Our regular haunt on the lower slopes of Costaccia is Berghütte, but it has had mixed reports recently. A reader favourite nearby is the newish Scialket, on skier's left of the Cassana gondola. Way the best place on Carosello is Tea da Cip e Ciop, on the lower slopes. In the middle of the Mottolino slopes, Camanel di Planon gets good reports, as do the rustic restaurants at the Trepalle and Passo d'Eira lift bases. The table-service Luciano's restaurant is a peaceful option in the big M'Eating Point.

More on the slopes

For beginners There are countless short drag-lifts ranged along the lower slopes of Costaccia/Carosello next to the village, and the occasional chair-lift. Some are on what we consider uncomfortably steep slopes, but the San Rocco chair and drag near the Carosello gondola are fine. Unfortunately, your next move probably needs to be to the north end of the village to ski the Cassana gondola or the higher Valandrea Vetta chair. Beginners pay for lifts by the ride, using points cards.

For true blue skiers There is some excellent blue skiing, but it is fragmented and doesn't add up to a lot. There are many better resorts than this for skiers lacking confidence.

At the top of Costaccia is a lovely gentle slope about a mile long served by a fast chair. There are shorter blue runs lower down, too, but to get down to them your choice is riding the Costaccia gondola or tackling a bit of a red run. Across the valley there are slightly more testing but still genuine blues from Mottolino to the gondola base and to Trepalle, on the back of the hill.

There's also a very gentle blue down the ridge from Monte della Neve to the Mottolino mid-mountain station, but there is no way for a blue-run skier to get to it since the removal (in about 2016) of the ancient (and admittedly uncomfortable) slow chair-lift along the ridge. Shame.

For the confident It's clear from the piste map that there is quite a lot of red-run skiing to do here. Practically all of it is worthwhile without being particularly testing, but for challenges you can look to the groomed blacks (read the following section). A favourite red is the 600m vertical one down the Mottolino gondola.

On the other hand, it has to be said that the slopes are a bit monotonous – the mountainsides are basically rather featureless. There are plenty of spots where you find two adjacent pistes that are difficult to distinguish.

For experts There are black pistes dotted around, and a bunch of three down the Monte della Neve chair-lift; most touch black gradients here and there, but are essentially tough reds (they are regularly groomed). The trickiest is at the bottom of Carosello – relatively narrow and steep, and prone to ice.

In the past Livigno has banned off-piste skiing and then tried to control it, but it now embraces it and goes out of its way to keep people safe. There's a safety briefing on Sunday evenings, a guide available for consultation every evening at the Outdoor Centre and a local avalanche bulletin produced every morning. Three areas (on Carosello, Costaccia and Mottolino) have been designated low-risk 'freeride approaching areas'.

There's quite a bit to do, with 900m/1000m verticals available on both sides of the valley. In the Mottolino sector there are worthwhile routes back towards Livigno and into Vallaccia to the east, both from the top of the lifts and from points a short hike south over the peak.

It's an attractive, traditional village, with a good chance of snow in the streets to complete the scene

In the Carosello sector, from the top of the Federia chair-lift there's an excellent descent down Val Cantone to the village, and hiking up to Pizzo Cantone or Monte delle Rezze opens up multiple longer options – shady runs towards Livigno and sunny runs ending at Campacciolo on the valley road.

Such is the change of heart about off-piste that there's even heli-skiing available now, at attractive prices. Search online for heliskiing Livigno and you'll be spoilt for choice.

Fancy stuff Mottolino produces its own 'Fun & Family' map, which presents quite a catalogue of terrain features – an impressive snow park that's claimed to be the biggest in Italy (four kicker lines, a jib line with 60 features, a huge air bag for experts only), a natural pipe, a moguls area, a 'freeride cross' area (which seems to combine freeride, freestyle and boardercross elements) and several fun parks aimed at kids.

On Carosello there are smaller snow parks at the top and bottom, a boardercross course and several kids' mini-parks near the village.

The resort

It's a pleasant and lively village, the endless main street lined by chalets, many stone-built, wood-built or wood-clad, many housing tempting shops displaying duty-free goods (to which an advertising-based guide is distributed). A long stretch of this main street is traffic-free.

Convenience It's easy to find lodgings near a key lift. The main concentrations of hotels are in two areas: the 1km stretch of the main street towards the north end of the village between the effective centre (directly opposite the Mottolino gondola) and the Cassana gondola, the northernmost lift; and a second 1km stretch to the south, ending with the Carosello gondola. There are also plenty of hotels across the valley at Teola, between the two Mottolino lift bases, too.

But wherever you are based you are likely to end up making heavy use of the good but complex system of free bus services, running on five lines (from 7am

to 8pm 'approximately') – plus shuttles between the two ski areas.

Lodgings There are over 20 4-star hotels, over 50 3-stars and even a handful of 2-star places. We've stayed happily in the 4-star Bivio near the Costaccia gondola, despite its popular cellar bar. Near the Carosello gondola, the cool 4-star Sporting takes some beating.

Bars and restaurants Afternoon action is mainly to be found on the sunny Mottolino side of the valley – notably at Camanel di Planon – though towards close of play the Carosello lift base is very lively (the Stalet claims to host the wildest parties in town). In the middle of the village, Diva Caffe is a lively and welcoming bar also doing good simple food. There are countless alternatives, mostly traditional in style; some are pictured and described in a free booklet. For a radical change, check out the cool Al Persef restaurant in the hotel Sporting, towards the south end.

Off the slopes The Aquagranda leisure centre/spa is an excellent facility, but located right on the northern edge of the village – 10,000m² divided into fun, relax and fitness areas, each including multiple pools. It's not cheap, and the fun area prices seem geared to those spending a whole day in the centre rather than an hour or two. There's a big outdoor ice rink at the north end of the village. A couple of the lifts on the lower slopes are used for sledging, and two others for tubing. There is a fair amount of cross-country skiing along the valley, rather less in the way of walks. There's a good range of other activities – snowmobiling, ice driving, ice climbing and so on.

For families It's a good place to bring young kids, provided you can identify a location that meets all your needs without a lot of bus rides. There are half a dozen snow gardens dotted along the village, and countless other opportunities to play on the snow. There are fun parks on the mountains aimed at kids.

More information

livigno.eu
carosello3000.com
mottolino.com
aquagrandalivigno.com

Bardonecchia

Not far west of Turin are the mountains forming the French border. Keep left at Oulx, and you reach Sauze; keep right for the Fréjus road and rail tunnels, and you come to Bardonecchia. It has skiing on much the same scale as Sauze, but without the further skiing that the Via Lattea offers Sauze visitors. It's a small valley town rather than a mountain village, unremarkable but pleasant, in a grand mountain setting. The altitude is on the low side – but so are the prices, even by Italian standards. The railway that laid its economic foundations can now bring skiers from London (via Paris), and road access is easy too (though not cheap).

The resort is popular with British school parties, so this is one Italian resort that isn't necessarily a great target for a half-term holiday.

The mountains in brief

Size Small enough to have a keen skier looking at excursions
Slopes Intermediate steepness, pleasantly wooded, decent vertical
Snow Snowfall record, altitude and orientation make it a bit unreliable
System, Lift Improving, but there is still a way to go
Sustenance Restaurants where you need them, and a few good spots
For beginners Good slopes at village level, and easy runs to progress to
For true blue skiers A fair amount to do, in both slope sectors
For the confident Entertaining hills, within the limits of their size
For experts Some good tree skiing, given good snow
Fancy stuff The remnants of the Olympic park beckon

Bardonecchia – the resort in brief

Convenience There are lodgings at the main lift; most people need a bus
Lodgings An adequate range, but nothing special
Bars and restaurants Livens up at weekends, but normally quiet
Off the slopes The options are adequate; Turin is easily reached by train
For families A viable destination if you stay near the main lift base

Pass notes	Key facts		Key ratings	
The 6-day pass covers a day in the Italian side of the Via Lattea and a day in Montgenèvre – you must claim a voucher before you travel. Beginners can buy points cards for the nursery lifts.	Altitude	1290m	Size	**
	Range	1290–2695m	Snow	**
	Slopes (see text)	100km	Fast lifts	**
	Where to stay, ideally		Mountain rest's	***
	At or near the Campo Smith lift station.		Beginner	***
			True blue	***
	Websites		Confident	****
	bardonecchia.it		Expert	**
	bardonecchiaski.com		Convenience	**
			Families	***
			Village charm	***

The mountains in detail

There are two mountains. The larger area has three chair-lift bases: on the south-west fringe of the town is Campo Smith; further out, at either end of the rustic village of Melezet, are Les Arnauds and Melezet. The skiing above Campo Smith and Les Arnauds is branded Colomion (the peak above the slopes), while the area as a whole has no name; we're going to call it Colomion-Melezet. A mile from Campo Smith, east of the town, across the railway, river and motorway, is smaller but taller Jafferau, with a gondola going up to a mid-mountain focus called Bardonecchia 2000 (actually at about 1940m) and chair-lifts and drags on the upper mountain.

With a car, outings to France are possible. The Fréjus tunnel takes you to numerous resorts in the Maurienne valley and the famous Trois Vallées. Heading south, you can visit Montgenèvre – possibly by train and bus.

Size

The resort claims 100km of pistes. If correct, this would put the area ahead of places like Livigno and Monterosa Ski, and it doesn't feel that big. Sure enough, a few minutes playing with measurements on Google maps, and comparisons with other resorts, are enough to confirm that the reality doesn't match the claim – we reckon it's nearer 50km than 100km – and justifies no more than a ✳✳ size rating.

Slopes

The mountains are essentially of red-run gradient, with blue runs cutting across the slopes. Colomion-Melezet is virtually all in the trees; Jafferau's top lifts are open.

Colomion-Melezet currently peaks at 2217m, giving a maximum vertical of over 800m. Jafferau is taller – about 2700m, not the 2807m marked on the map. Still, it offers a quite impressive 1350m vertical over about 6km, snow permitting.

Snow

Not a strong point. Like nearby Sauze, Bardonecchia doesn't have a great snowfall record, and at about 1300m the resort altitude is distinctly on the low side for this part of the Alps. Campo Smith is fairly shady, but Jafferau faces more or less due west, and the lower slopes suffer accordingly in the afternoon. About 40% of the pistes are covered by snowmaking – on Jafferau just the one run from mid-mountain to the base, but lots of runs on Colomion-Melezet. A different problem is

that the top of Jafferau is quite exposed, and can be adversely affected by strong, cold winds.

System, Lift

It's not a great picture, though it is improving. On the major sector, the access lifts at Campo Smith and Melezet are fast quads, but the three chairs on the upper mountain are slow – as is the access chair at Les Arnauds. The key lifts on the upper mountain, in fact, are drags a mile long. We hear that a new quad chair is being installed on the upper slopes above Melezet in 2019, replacing both the Sellette double chair and the Seba drag. The piste map also shows two further lifts 'in preparation', to replace lifts recently removed. At present it's not clear whether or when they will go ahead.

At Jafferau, above the gondola from the base, the ancient double chair-lift at mid-mountain was replaced by a fast six-seater in 2017. The Ban chair, going to the high point, is a slow double. Note that the alternative Jafferau drag has no piste anywhere nearby – best not to fall off.

On weekdays away from the peak weeks, the slopes are pleasantly quiet. At half-term there may be lots of British kids, and French school holidays have an impact, too. Italians are brought out from Turin by the carnival period up to Shrove Tuesday, and by weekend sunshine. The Campo Smith lift gets busy then.

Sustenance

There are restaurants at each of the four mid-mountain lift stations – La Grangia above Campo Smith gets good reports. And there are a couple of good spots higher up – La Capannina on Jafferau, and Punta Colomion, at the top of the long Colomion drag, with a warm welcome from the Anglo-Italian owners.

More on the slopes

For beginners

There are valley-level nursery slopes on a row of lifts at Campo Smith and a single lift at Melezet, and a single lift at mid-mountain on Jafferau – handy but doubtless busy when snow at village level is poor. All these gentle slopes are shown on the map in green – extremely unusual in Italy. You pay by means of points cards.

On both mountains there are easy longer runs to move on to.

Colomion-Melezet, the bigger of the two slope sectors, is pretty much wooded from top to bottom

For true blue skiers

Blue-run skiers are quite well catered for here, though not quite as well as you might think from a quick glance at the piste map – closer inspection reveals that lots of blue runs around mid-mountain on Colomion-Melezet are accessed only by skiing red or even black runs.

Even so, there are good runs to be done above and below Chesal, above Melezet, and on the lower slopes at both Campo Smith and Les Arnauds.

On Jafferau, there's a blue of 1000m vertical from the top all the way to the bottom of the Challier drag-lift, which you ride back up to Bardonecchia 2000.

For confident intermediates

Within the constraints of the small area, there is lots for a red-run skier to do, particularly on Colomion-Melezet if the snow is good to the base stations – satisfying top-to-bottom runs at Campo Smith and Les Arnauds, with variants on the upper mountain; and worthwhile runs on the upper part of the two-stage Chesal chair at Melezet. There are good runs on Jafferau, too, with a descent of 760m vertical from the top to the mid-station.

Bear in mind the risk of poor snow on the lower slopes, and the many slow lifts.

For experts

There are bits of black piste marked on the map, and bits of 'unmarked and not maintained' trail; the latter are about the steepest pitches on the mountains, but even these don't reach black gradient.

There is off-piste terrain to be explored beside the pistes on the open upper slopes, particularly on Jafferau, and some interesting wooded terrain on both mountains – some lovely gladed areas, as well as tighter trees. You can ski off the back of Jafferau into Val Fredda, ending up at the village of Rochemolles.

Fancy stuff

There is a terrain park on the upper mountain above Melezet. Given its Olympic heritage, the park naturally has some impressive features, but it also has beginner terrain. The Olympic half-pipe is no longer in operation.

Bardonecchia – the resort

Bardonecchia's setting is splendid, with 3000m peaks to the west, north and east; it's a popular base for active summer holidays. But it is a rather plain little town, centred on the arrow-straight 700m-long main street, lined by restaurants and shops of all kinds, running from the railway station towards the cobbled streets and handsome church of the old town. Although skiing has gone on here for over a century, the place lacks ski resort atmosphere (no bad thing, for some). Spacious, wooded suburbs spread towards the Campo Smith lift base.

Convenience

We see no reason to stay in the centre, but if you do you'll certainly want to use the free ski-buses linking the town and the lift bases – the central area is about 1km from Campo Smith. Services beyond Campo Smith are less frequent.

Lodgings

Right on the snow (you hope) at Campo Smith is the big, unusually styled 4-star hotel Rivè. But we're inclined towards the smaller, more personal 4-star Cà Fiore, only a short walk away across the river. There are cheaper options, and apartment residences, including a big one in the hotel Rivè complex. If planning to stay in the town, beware noise from trains. Sempre Ski operates a 20-bed catered chalet between the centre and Campo Smith – away from the railway – and represents a couple of simple hotels.

Out of the ordinary
Up at Bardonecchia 2000 is the 4-star hotel Jafferau. Great views.

Bars and restaurants

The Chesal mountain restaurant advertises après action with the tag 'Crazy Chesal'; we haven't witnessed it, sadly, but we've seen pics of musicians performing. Harald's at Campo Smith gets lively at teatime. Our friends at Sempre

Ski tell us that Lalimentari, nearby, is a must for an aperitivo.

There are lots of traditional, unpretentious restaurants, clustered around Campo Smith, along the main street in the town, and a handful in the old town. For something different, take a snowcat way up the valley beyond Melezet to the rustic Rifugio I Re Magi. Or go up to Punta Colomion and ski down after dinner with head torches.

Off the slopes

Close to Campo Smith are an artificial outdoor skating rink and an indoor swimming pool, also housing a sauna and gym, and tennis courts. A sled-on-rails coaster opened in 2019 at Campo Smith,

about 1km long. There's tubing on one of the Baby lifts at Campo Smith.

At Pian del Colle, 5km away up the valley beyond Melezet, there are cross-country ski trails of various difficulties – plus a 20km itinerary going on up the valley, climbing to 1800m. There's a trail from Bardonecchia 2000, too. You can go snowshoeing in the same areas, and at other points up on the ski slopes.

For families

Choose lodgings at or near Campo Smith and, provided you get snow at village level to play in, you should have a satisfactory time. In 2019 sledging on the floodlit nursery slope was introduced (conveniently close to Harald's bar).

A good view of the town, even if it includes a long-dead chair-lift – our photo options were limited

Cervinia

Cervinia / Valtournenche + Zermatt (Switzerland)

There is nowhere quite like Cervinia – high, open, sunny, gentle, perfectly groomed slopes by the mile, under the peak of the mighty Cervino (aka Matterhorn). It suits some people perfectly and others, of course, not at all.

From the slopes, the village is a blot on the landscape, and is showing little sign of improvement, but it is quite pleasant and enjoyable to inhabit.

Part of the appeal for some is the skiing over the Swiss border, above Zermatt. But Cervinia isn't the ideal starting point, and there are other snags, discussed later. Among these is the risk of closure of the top lifts by high wind. (This can affect the top Cervinia slopes as well as the link.)

You may see the name prefaced by 'Breuil', the pre-Mussolini name.

The mountains in brief

Size A good size – huge if you pay the premium to access Zermatt

Slopes Glorious cruising on long, open slopes offering decent verticals

Snow Good conditions are the norm, once the base is in place

System, Lift Some flaws, mainly above Valtournenche

Sustenance Several good spots, with further treats over in Zermatt

For beginners Fine – good slopes at village level and mid-mountain

For true blue skiers Great, once you've figured which reds are fake

For the confident Less good than the map suggests; but there's Zermatt ...

For experts Much more interesting than most people think

Fancy stuff The park's impressive, and easily reached

Cervinia – the resort in brief

Convenience Walks are mostly bearable, and there are some ski-in places

Lodgings A catered chalet and a Club Med add to the usual options

Bars and restaurants Not a riot, but there is après-ski life in the village

Off the slopes An improving range of diversions, but as yet no aqua-centre

For families Viable – handy nursery slopes with kids' snow garden

Pass notes	Key facts		Key ratings	
Passes for 3+ days cover other Aosta Valley resorts – but it's a long drive down to the valley. A daily extension for Zermatt cost €34 in 2018; upgrading to a full international pass cost about twice that. Beginners can buy cheap day passes covering two beginner lifts and one trip up to Plan Maison to use the nursery lift there.	Altitude	2050m	Size	*****
	Range	1565–3820m	Snow	****
	Slopes (see text)	360km	Fast lifts	****
			Mountain rest's	****
	Where to stay, ideally		Beginner	*****
	Within walking distance of the Cretaz chair-lift or the Plan Maison gondola.		True blue	****
			Confident	***
	Websites		Expert	***
	cervinia.it		Convenience	***
	skilife.ski		Families	***
			Village charm	**

The mountains in detail

Cervinia's own slopes fall into two main identifiable sectors. First: a gondola and a rarely used cable car rise 500m to the restaurant/lift complex of Plan Maison; from there, a chain of chair-lifts goes up to the Swiss border at Theodulpass, accessing a web of runs back to Plan Maison with links to skier's right across to the area around Plan Torrette, also accessed by a six-seat chair-lift from the village. From Plan Maison a gondola goes off to the second sector around Laghi Cime Bianche; from there, a cable car goes up to Testa Grigia, also on the border, start of the famously long Ventina run to the village. Branching left from the Ventina run you can ride a short chair-lift to access the slopes of Valtournenche, 9km down the valley and 500m lower.

Beyond the Swiss border are Zermatt's long and gentle glacier slopes – read our feature panel, over the page. Zermatt is building a big gondola from Testa Grigia to Klein Matterhorn at the very top. A plan to build an 8km gondola from the Monterosa area seems to be gaining support.

Size

Cervinia is now a bit coy about its size. Zermatt is less so: 360km for the whole shared area, it proclaims. Of course, Christoph Schrahe is on hand to detect that this figure certainly incorporates some multiplication (read the intro to the book). But this is all a bit academic: the area is clearly one of the biggest in the Alps, and merits a ***** rating. Without Zermatt, it rates only ***.

Slopes

The terrain is mostly gentle, steepening towards the top and bottom. There are some trees on the small Cielo Alto slopes south of the village, but the main area is treeless. The local slopes are sunny, mostly facing south of west, so it's no surprise that Cervinia has to rely on Zermatt for glacier skiing. (At the very top of the Ventina run there is a tiny patch of more or less permanent snow.)

There are some very long runs – from Klein Matterhorn it's over 1800m vertical to Cervinia. It's a world-class 2250m down to Valtournenche, but the descent is spoilt by a short chair-lift ride near the top of the Valtournenche area. At Testa Grigia you are about 6km from Cervinia, and over 8km from Valtournenche.

The piste map marks 'freeride' runs on the Swiss side, with no further explanation. The Swiss map, to add to the confusion, gives them the label 'freeriding pistes'. Zermatt confirms that they are marked, avalanche-safe and patrolled. They are, in other words, ungroomed pistes. Read the book's intro for more on this chaotic situation.

Snow

The area's west-south-west orientation is a theoretical weakness (the slopes get the sun at the warmest time of day), but the altitude – you spend most of your time skiing above the 2500m mark – and the location on the Alpine watershed ensure low temperatures and good snowfalls, particularly above mid-mountain.

Snowmaking covers most of the main runs, but it has to be said there are serious gaps in the coverage – the black runs are not covered, but more importantly quite a few reds are not. So a drought can limit what's open, and it's a better bet for late holidays than for early ones. All in all, you'd be very unlucky to encounter snow problems here, and on our many visits we've always enjoyed excellent conditions.

System, Lift

Fast lifts dominate, although some are now quite old. Nursery lifts apart, the only slow lifts above Cervinia are the short double chair-lift serving the little Cielo Alto sector, close to the village, and the mile-long Lago Goillet triple chair offering one way to the Valtournenche slopes (which can be avoided). Both the chair-liftss up from mid-mountain Salette at Valtournenche are slow, too.

As in so many Italian resorts, invasions from the northern cities on sunny weekends can be a problem, but otherwise queues are rare, and on weekdays it's possible to find deserted pistes even in February. The first chair-lift out of Plan Maison can be a bit of a bottleneck – it's a quad, 20 years old, and needs to be upgraded. At busy times, seek peace on the powerful Pancheron six-pack above Plan Torrette, or use the Laghi Cime Bianche lifts to the top.

Sustenance

There are plenty of restaurants, marked but not named on the piste map, including a couple right at the top, on the border – the Teodulo is worth checking out.

Our regular haunt is Chalet Etoile, in the middle of the blue runs above Plan Maison. Despite high prices it is very popular, and can be busy when other places are not. It's best on a fine day, when the terrace is quite relaxed and the pressure is taken off the tightly spaced tables indoors. Further up the hill, Bontadini has an excellent reputation, but we've somehow never managed to pay a visit. Maybe next time. The Igloo on the Ventina piste gets good reports, too.

The glorious Ventina piste – justifiably red at this point near the top, but an easy cruise for much of its length

Other reader tips include Baita Cretaz just above the village ('great food, reasonable prices'), Plan Torrette ('our favourite – great food, amazing views') and Tuktu at Plan Maison ('no frills but good food and proper toilets', 'good food, great view, music late afternoon').

At Valtournenche, the relatively new Foyer des Guides, well down the home run, is a splendid stone-and-wood chalet doing excellent food – usually busy, even in low season.

Zermatt's mountain restaurants are famously wonderful, and some of the best are on the way down to Zermatt from Cervinia, around Furi. Try Marmottes, Aroleid or Silvana above Furi, Furri at Furi, or Zum See or Blatten lower down.

The Swiss connection

If you already know Zermatt, when visiting Cervinia you'll probably want to renew your acquaintance with the resort. If you don't know it, and you're a confident, strong skier who somehow has been compelled to book a holiday in Cervinia, you shouldn't miss the chance to devote a day or two to exploration of what this great resort has to offer.

At the border you are in the middle of Zermatt's least interesting slopes, on its exceptionally long glacier. But it doesn't take long to drop 500m and get down to much more challenging runs, above and below Trockener Steg and Schwarzsee – genuine red pistes and 'freeride' runs, often seriously mogulled.

From Furi, 1600m vertical below Testa Trigia, a gondola goes across the valley to Riffelberg with a chair-lift going on to a point below Gornergrat for some of the best skiing in Zermatt. And from there chair-lifts take you on to the Sunnegga and Rothorn sectors, with further excellent red pistes and 'freeride' routes.

Challenging skiing isn't the only attraction. Zermatt's numerous mountain restaurants are the best in the world. But with the Swiss franc costing over 80p they are very expensive. And you must be careful not to linger too long over lunch; allow for queues on the way back, and watch the weather – although the high, exposed link is now less vulnerable to wind, thanks to the new 3S gondola to Klein Matterhorn.

Timid blue-run skiers should note: the Ventina piste 7 back from Testa Grigia is a genuine red until it becomes 7.0; red piste 6 via Theodulpass is not steep but a bit narrow at the start. If in doubt, ride down.

Testa Grigia, with the gentle Zermatt glacier slopes on the left – seen from Furggsattel, also on the border

More on the slopes

For beginners

There is a good slope right next to the village, served by a free carpet-lift and the 450m Campetto quad chair-lift, and another slope up at Plan Maison served by the 480m Vieille button lift. The special beginner day pass covers both of these lifts, and one return trip on the gondola to reach Plan Maison. Free lifts would be better, but this deal is a great advance on a full lift pass. The blue slopes above Plan Maison are ideal for progression.

For true blue skiers

As noted above, there are lovely, easy blues at mid-mountain. The blue run back to the village has a slightly stiffer stretch in the lower part; more importantly, it is the main way back to the village, so it gets busy and chopped up.

With growing confidence you might find these blues a bit tame, but fear not: there are also red runs of essentially blue gradient to move on to. Among them are 46 and 6 from the Bontadini chair, and 7.0 from Laghi Cime Bianche.

So there is quite a bit to do, and some long descents to be made.

If you don't mind slow lifts, it's worth taking a bus down to Valtournenche, where there are good blues at Salette, at mid-mountain. (Access from Cervinia on skis involves genuine red runs.)

For confident intermediates

For keen, competent skiers there are three key lifts.

The cable car to Testa Grigia serves the top part of the famous Ventina run, down to Laghi Cime Bianche, which is a genuine red (the second half of this top part was classified black until about 2016). In the morning it's usually a very enjoyable blast, but later it can be heavily moguled. Below Laghi Cime Bianche the run mellows to a cruise. Peel off on to 13 to reach 16 for a bit more of a challenge.

Secondly, the reds on the fast Pancheron chair are genuine, and nicely varied – and there is the bonus of easy blacks to try out on skier's right of the lift.

Thirdly, the fast chair at the top of the Valtournenche sector serves a set of worthwhile reds. There's also a cracking long descent from top to bottom of the area on piste 1 – over 1000m vertical, much of it well away from lifts.

The reds on the Lago Goillet chair are good stuff, but the slow chair is a pain.

The village is no rustic beauty, and the suburbs up the hill are not much better; but it's quite a setting

For experts

There is hardly any steep piste skiing. From the Pancheron chair-lift, piste 59 starts with a genuine black stretch, but soon mellows, and 62 below it is essentially a tough red which also has the drawback that it misses the Pancheron lift base, and sends you down to the village to ride the lower Cretaz chair. Pity. Piste 5bis is another black of tough red gradient. The short blacks at Cielo Alto barely deserve the classification. But the off-piste possibilities are something else.

There is quite a bit of underused terrain accessible from the Pancheron chair, and some trickier routes below Plan Maison. But the real tests are higher up.

To skier's left of the red runs from Theodulpass there are two well-known options. Close to the Bontadini chair is the line of a now-defunct black piste. We guess the piste was abandoned because of the dangerous cliffs to skier's left. Then there are much more demanding routes further left, from Theodulpass and on both sides of Testa Grigia; lower down these routes divide to go left to Laghi Cime Bianche, or to go on down past Lago Goillet to the village.

The Cervino Alpine guides' society offers quite a range of adventures. One is to descend the Unterer Theodulgletscher, on skier's right of the glacier pistes. Another is to traverse from Furggsattel to the disused Furggen cable car station (decommissioned in the early 1990s) to descend 900m to Plan Maison. The guides do heli-trips, too, sometimes with descent to Zermatt.

Fancy stuff

At 2800m, above Plan Maison, Indianpark is said to be the highest snow park in Europe. It's a good size – 400m long and 100m wide – with some serious kickers but also beginner-friendly features. There's also a quite serious boardercross course.

Cervinia – the resort

Cervinia doesn't have the iconic view of the Matterhorn that Zermatt enjoys, but it does have a dramatic setting close to the mountain. It's a rather messy place, with not much sense of planning (and little evidence of its roots as a climbing village), but the towny main street is traffic-free and lively, and its buildings have some traditional style.

Convenience

It's not a big place – the main part of the village is about 800m end to end. The direct lifts to Plan Maison start an irritating climb above the south end of the village, and there is a lot to be said for choosing a base towards the north end, where you'll have easy access to the less direct Cretaz chair-lift. There are also lodgings in developments detached from the village, up the hills to the east and south (in an area called Cielo Alto); these have nearby pistes going down to one lift or another. So there are some slope-side lodgings.

A bus service runs every 20 minutes (10 at peak times) through the southern end of the resort and up to the gondola station. Every half hour (mostly) a bus runs up to the Cielo Alto area and then down to the gondola station.

Lodgings

It's not a notably swanky resort – the hotel scene is dominated by the 25 3-star places – but a number of upscale 4-star places have opened in recent years to give the 5-star Relais & Chateaux Hermitage a bit of competition. There are also about 10 2-stars hotels.

Following our own advice in the previous section, on our last visit we stayed near the Cretaz lift at the 4-star hotel Excelsior Planet – a lovely two-storey room with stunning Matterhorn views, and an excellent dinner. On the previous occasion, we enjoyed staying at the 4-star Saint Hubertus Resort – a stylish, welcoming apartment-hotel, a short walk above the village and the gondola; superb food, charming service.

There's a Club Med up the hill south of the village; not one of their best, but in a ski-in location. Inghams has the no-nonsense 25-bed chalet hotel Dragon in a great central location at the foot of the slopes (with a popular bar). It also has two hotels exclusively contracted.

Bars and restaurants

Like so many Italian resorts, the place is pretty quiet midweek, but even so you can find animated bars. It livens up at weekends when the Italians arrive.

On the mountain, the après bar of the cool hotel Principe delle Nevi is a tempting place to pause on your final descent of red piste 3. In the village, the hotel Samovar's tea room is a bit of an institution, but it also has a cosy bar. The woody bars of the hotel Grivola get pretty lively. Inghams' chalet hotel Dragon has a popular bar, naturally very British. The Copa Pan is an old favourite too – for straightforward food as well as drinks. La Grotta is a good all-round restaurant/pizzeria, but for pizza Sotto Zero takes some beating. For a serious meal the top hotels are all worth considering, but there are other options – Un Mare di Neve and Wood, for example.

Off the slopes

This is certainly not a great resort for non-skiers, but there's now a reasonable range of off-slope activities. At the foot of the slopes in front of Lino's bar is a small natural ice rink, open until midnight; curling can be arranged. In rather bleak surroundings at the entrance to the village there's a 3km cross-country loop; for more choice, in a more hospitable setting, head down to Valtournenche. As well as a couple of identified footpaths there are signposted snowshoe trails up on the slopes, and 'off-piste' routes down at Valtournenche. There is dog sledding nearby, and a good range of snowmobiling excursions.

For families

The resort has attractions, with a long stretch of nursery slope next to the village (and a choice of lodgings nearby) incorporating a snow garden and carpet-lift, and another carpet-lift up at Plan Maison. For swimming, look to your hotel, or to Valtournenche.

Valtournenche

Valtournenche is 500m lower than Cervinia and not surprisingly in a much less bleak setting, well below the treeline. It's pleasantly traditional in style, with a fine church bell tower at its heart, but it spreads for about a mile along the road to Cervinia, so it's no rustic idyll. Buses between the resorts run about every hour.

The access gondola base (and the arrival point of the piste from mid-mountain) is the best part of a mile north of the centre. A ski-bus runs from the village every 20 minutes. Getting up to the top of the Valtournenche slopes, to access the Cervinia slopes, takes some time; but the local slopes have attractions.

Above Salette at mid-mountain there are good blue runs, not accessible from Cervinia without skiing genuine reds. And the long red to the lift base is mostly in the trees, offering the best skiing in this area on a bad weather day. It has snowmaking to the bottom. There's also an excellent Wild West children's area at Salette, with three carpet-lifts.

The busy through-road rather spoils the village, and it's pretty lifeless in the evening. But there are some decent simple hotels at sub-Cervinia prices – about 16 of them, 3-star and 2-star.

As noted above, there are walks with and without snowshoes. An advantage over Cervinia is there's a small sports centre in the village with a laned swimming pool plus sauna, a climbing wall and basketball/volleyball courts.

Cortina d'Ampezzo

Cortina fits none of the standard Alpine resort patterns. It is a big-time racing resort – it's hosting the Alpine World Ski Championships in 2021 (mid-February), and in 2026 many of the Alpine Olympics races (70 years on from 1956, when Cortina hosted the whole winter games). But it is a polished little town, not a mountain village – Italy's most fashionable resort, by some margin. Many of its Italian weekend visitors are here not to ski but to relax, lunch in the sun and shop – and perhaps to enjoy some walking amid the spectacular Dolomite peaks that surround the resort.

The skiing is interestingly varied and crowd-free, as well as scenic, but very fragmented. To enjoy it you really need to get into a relaxed frame of mind and accept the schlepping around by bus or car.

The mountains in brief

Size On the small side, especially for a keen, competent piste-basher, but ...

Slopes Wide variety, including plenty of challenges and some trees

Snow Good snowmaking makes up for the usual erratic Dolomite snowfall

System, Lift Some upgrades in progress, but still some irritating slow lifts

Sustenance Recommendable places in all the main sectors

For beginners Excellent arrangements in two sectors, either side of town

For true blue skiers Not ideal, but quite a bit to do, in several sectors

For the confident Given good snow, an interesting and challenging area

For experts Pray for powder, and pay for guidance

Fancy stuff The park won't amuse experts, but is OK for the rest of us

Cortina – the resort in brief

Convenience The bus services work; get used to using them

Lodgings Something for everyone, including the budget-conscious

Bars and restaurants A wide choice, from trad to cool; some involve taxis

Off the slopes Lots to do, from Olympic skating to world-class shopping

For families Good facilities, but not much sledging-from-the door lodging

---

Pass notes	Key facts		Key ratings	
A pass is available for Cortina plus several small outlying areas. The extra cost of a Superski pass, covering the Sella Ronda and other areas, is small. There is no special pass for beginners – you pay by the ride, or buy points cards until you are confident about buying a full pass.	Altitude	1200m	Size	**
	Range	1200–2828m	Snow	***
	Slopes (see text)	100km	Fast lifts	***
	Where to stay, ideally		Mountain rest's	****
	Within strolling distance of the main circular bus route, #8.		Beginner	****
			True blue	***
			Confident	****
	Websites		Expert	***
	dolomiti.org		Convenience	*
	impianticortina.it		Families	**
	faloriacristallo.it		Village charm	***
	freccianelcielo.com			

The mountains in detail

Cortina's skiing is antiquated as well as fragmented. The one six-seat chair-lift is almost 15 years old; as we write, the resort's first gondola is being built, replacing the 50-year-old cable car to Col Druscè where a relatively modern cable car goes on up to the Ra Valles sector (aka Tofana). A mile away, across town, a 40-year-old cable car gently ferries 600 people an hour up to Faloria, from the far side of which a short walk brings you to the very small Cristallo sector. Buses link these lifts and the biggest and most varied sector, variously known as Socrepes, Pocol or Pomedes. This can also be reached via a black descent from Ra Valles.

Two furthers linked sectors, Cinque Torri and Lagazuoi, are way west of the town. The bus from the Pocol slopes takes 10 minutes; a 5km gondola is being planned. No waiting, but slower. Buy more buses instead?

Mietres, the little backwater area with slow chairs to the north of the town, has closed, with no prospect of revival.

Size

The resort generally claims to offer 120km of pistes, but this includes various small outlying areas – Misurina, San Vito di Cadore and Auronzo. Some years back Christoph Schrahe published a figure of about 70km for the areas next to the town – that is, not including Cinque Torri/ Lagazuoi, for which 29km are claimed. All things considered, we reckon a realistic total would be a bit under 100km, producing a ✳✳ size rating.

Slopes

The mountains offer a lot of variety, with something to suit everybody. There's more skiing on open slopes above the trees than within them; the lower part of Faloria is the place to be in bad weather. It's possible to construct some big descents – over 1000m vertical from Pomedes to the village, and over 1600m from the top lift on Ra Valles. (This is the Bus Tofana double chair-lift to 2828m, not the top cable car, which goes much

higher for the amusement of summer tourists, not skiers.) But you spend most of your time doing more modest verticals – maybe 750m on Pomedes, 350m on Faloria. The Lagazuoi cable car rises 650m, with a splendid red back to the base; the 'hidden valley' run off the back drops about 1000m over about 6km.

There are some short green runs marked on the map in the Socrepes sector. We and some readers jumped to the obvious conclusion that the resort had adopted the French convention of marking very easy runs in green, but we were wrong (and one reader at least was distressed as a result). The most recent piste map has no explanation, but on earlier maps they are defined as 'not controlled ski tracks'. We've checked, and they are indeed not formally patrolled.

This is absurd for several reasons. We've conveyed this view to the resort.

Snow

The Dolomites area as a whole has an erratic snow record, depending on weather from the Adriatic which is less reliable than weather from the Atlantic. That's why the resorts in the region became so good at snowmaking. The bottom line is that you can't count on powder, but you can count on most of the skiing being open, and enjoyable.

As always, it's the sunny steep slopes that are the most liable to problems in sunny weather – strong sun, not easy to groom. The classic example here is the black Forcella Rossa, the link from Ra Valles to Pomedes, which faces directly south, more or less.

System, Lift

The lift system is adequate rather than impressive. There are fast chair-lifts in most of the key positions, but also quite a lot of slow lifts dotted around.

The 50-year-old cable car from the ice rink to Col Drusciè, for access to Ra Valles, is being replaced as we write by a 10-person gondola with a mid-station near Colfiere (so it also replaces the slightly less venerable double chair from there).

In 2020 two slow lifts up at Ra Valles – the triple Pian Ra Valles and double Bus Tofana up to the area high point – are to be replaced by a two-stage fast quad with bubbles. But there are no current plans to replace the slow chairs elsewhere.

The infamous Forcella Staunies double chair in the Cristallo sector was retired in 2016, at 60 years old, chopping 100m off Cortina's top height. A replacement is apparently proposed, but not approved.

The planned gondola between Pocol and Cinque Torri should go out to tender in 2019 and be built in 2020, in theory.

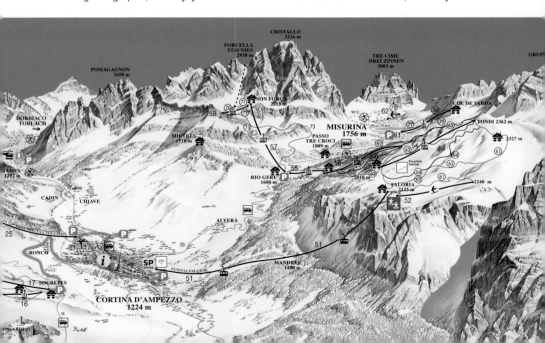

Queues are not generally a problem, but can arise at popular lifts on sunny weekends. The Lagazuoi cable car is about halfway between Cortina and Alta Badia, and naturally attracts skiers from both – it can be very busy on a fine day.

Sustenance

Restaurants are mostly not named on the piste map. The topo map on the back of the panoramic map is more helpful. There are good places in most sectors.

Our traditional favourite is on Faloria – Capanna Tondi, a little way below the top on red piste 61. It has a series of small, cosy rooms within, great views from the terrace and a wide range of dishes, served by friendly staff.

At the top of Pomedes, the eponymous restaurant is a lovely place; we haven't tried the food. At Col Druscié, the 1778 restaurant gets good reports; lacking a reservation, we couldn't get a table when we visited. A new wine bar/restaurant has been opened alongside the 1778 by Masi, a big name in production of Amarone etc.

We haven't been for years, but El Camineto, below Rumerlo, is apparently still top-notch – good enough to draw a full house up the hill for dinner, as well as a few for lunch. When we had lunch there [cough] years ago, we were the only people who had arrived on skis.

At the top of Cinque Torri, Rifugio Averau is a great spot – excellent food served with good humour even when the place is rammed, and great views.

Stop press We hear that the comatose Baita Piè Tofana at Rumerlo has been revived – and it looks very promising.

More on the slopes

For beginners

There are gentle beginner slopes at the bottom of the Socrepes sector, served by a 320m slow chair-lift. And immediately above it there are long, gentle runs to progress to. These are excellent arrangements; with a bit more altitude and more convenient lodgings, it would be perfect. Good luck in choosing a ski school; at the last count, there were eight.

For true blue skiers

There's quite a bit to do, but there are quite large areas of the mountains that are off-limits to a timid skier.

The Socrepes sector a mile or two out of town is blue-run HQ: a superb area for

It's well worth making the trip out to the Lagazuoi cable car, even if you resist the long 'hidden valley' run

relaxed skiing and building confidence, with nicely varied terrain, lightly wooded in places, served by two fast chair-lifts and a short, slow quad. But it's not huge.

Once you've built that confidence a bit, consider riding the Tofana Express chair and the Duca d'Aosta chair to ski Tofanina, a glorious blue over 4km long that curls away to skier's right of the lifts; it's a mix of genuine blue skiing, straight schussing and one tricky zigzag stretch that's not seriously steep but will certainly slow you down a bit.

The blues on and around Col Druscie should be approached with caution. They are basically a means of getting from A to B, where B can be the village. They are not steep, but mostly narrow; in good snow with no crowds, they can be very enjoyable – one reader called the descent to the village 'a highlight'. If they are busy, or icy, or both, they can be intimidating. But changes are afoot, triggered by the new gondola.

There is some pleasant blue skiing to be done at Col Gallina, near the base of the Lagazuoi cable car, but beware the blue run on the lower mountain at Cinque Torri; towards the end it is steeper than the adjacent genuine red.

If you're tempted to join your red-skiing mates on Faloria, you should be OK on the Tondi piste (61) – it's the gentlest of red runs; but it is quite short.

Don't be tempted by the blues on Ra Valles unless you are happy to take some stretches of red gradient in your stride.

For confident intermediates

This is an interesting, varied area, but keen competent skiers are likely to be unimpressed by its limited overall extent and fragmented nature.

Shady Faloria is excellent, provided you are up to runs at the easy end of the black spectrum; one of them, the top part of the lovely, away-from-all-lifts Vitelli, was classified red in the past (the bottom part still is red). Many of the runs are of rather limited vertical (Vitelli being an exception).

Across the road at Cristallo, the closure of the Staunies chair has removed a good run from the mid-station as well as the serious black from the top, but the area is still worth the occasional visit, particularly for a peaceful escape from weekend crowds on Faloria. The run back to the lift base is an excellent red.

Practically all the skiing up at Ra Valles is worthwhile – the blues have stretches that are distinctly red – but there's not much of it. The altitude and orientation mean that the snow is reliably good. Don't be tempted to try the black Forcella Rossa unless you have reliable evidence that it's in good shape (read the next section).

The Pomedes sector is superb when the snow is good (again, read the next section), with the sequence of two chairs below and above Duca d'Aosta offering 750m vertical and a choice of roughly four ways down.

The bus ride to Cinque Torri (10 min from the bus stop on skier's right of the Pocol area) is well worthwhile, for good shady runs on the fast chair on the lower front side and wide views on the run down to Fedare on the back. And do ride the Lagazuoi cable car – fab views, excellent red run to the base, long and wonderfully scenic 'hidden valley' run off the back down to Armentarola on the fringe of Alta Badia, where you can be dragged to lifts by horses (or call a taxi).

For experts

There is quite a bit of challenging piste skiing; difficulty depends heavily on snow conditions.

The map now includes a table of average and maximum gradients of the blacks – an excellent move. To our slight surprise, this shows the steepest to be Forcella Rossa, the link from Ra Valles to the lower areas – 32° at its steepest. Unfortunately it is also the sunniest, and when icy and mogulled it can be the stuff of nightmares; when groomed and soft it can be an amusing blast, and you can enjoy its fab views across Cortina. Our last three visits have delivered two blasts and one absolute nightmare.

Lower down, piste 41 (A) from Col Druscie and the runs at the top of Pomedes have proper black stretches, too. Catch these east-facing runs when they have been softened by the morning sun, and they can be delightful. Catch them in the afternoon, when they get very crisp, and it can be a different story. Vertigine Bianca is reckoned to be the second-steepest (31°) and is not groomed (except when it's a race course).

On shady Faloria, snow is more reliably good, and all the black pistes are at the easy end of the spectrum – and sure enough, the piste map lists maxima of 26° or 27° for most. Piste 68 was new in 2019, and carried signs warning of a gradient of 55% (29°) – and indeed it does have one short proper black stretch.

Forcella Staunies at the top of Cristallo, currently off-piste (read 'System, Lift'), is appreciably steeper than any of the remaining pistes. We haven't skied it, but topo maps suggest gradients near the top of well over 35°.

Cortina has a surprising range of off-piste runs; a few are quite tame, many are very demanding, either in terms of skiing or access, some involving crampons and/or ropes, fixed or not. Some of the descents are long – 1500m to 2000m vertical. When planning a trip, bear in mind the modest snow record.

On Cristallo, you currently have to climb to Staunies either to ski the steep but straightforward couloir you've climbed, or to tackle some very much more ambitious projects on the front or back side of Cristallo.

On Ra Valles the Bus chair accesses a long traverse north above rocky cliffs to the Vallon de Ra Ola, a fine, shady couloir followed by a long skate or walk to Fiames for a bus home. In the opposite direction, a half-hour hike and a spot of

mountaineering brings you to the Bus itself – a hole through the ridge; on the back of the mountain is a broad, sunny couloir, for a descent to Pomedes.

From the top of Faloria or from the Tondi drag-lift you can ski the long, easy Val Orita to Acquabona for a bus home. Peeling left from the Tondi piste gets you into the more demanding Sci 18 run, down to the cable car mid-station.

From the Lagazuoi cable car, with just a bit of climbing there is a wide range of options facing south and west, from some relatively easy ones (notably Col dei Bos) to some extremely tricky ones. At Cinque Torri, from Rifugio Scoiatolli there are easy routes north to the Passo Falzarego road and (much longer) east to the Passo Giau road. From the top chair-lift and the Croda Negra chair there are off-piste options.

Fancy stuff

In the past there has been a sizeable Snowpark on skier's left of the Socrepes slopes, and as we write in 2019 there are plans to revive it – but these plans are not definite. The smaller Freestyle Station on Faloria seems to be more of a fixture; it consists largely of rails, but it includes a half-pipe and its major feature appears to be a big air bag.

Cortina is ringed by spectacular Dolomite peaks; this is Tofana, with the Pomedes slopes left of centre

Cortina – the resort

Cortina spreads widely across its broad, beautiful valley, but life revolves around the long, curving, pedestrian Corso Italia in the centre, lined by shops, tea rooms, bars, hotels and ... shops. When we walk back to our hotel at teatime, we're the only ones carrying skis; everyone else is already in smart gear, and carrying bags full of (presumably) even smarter gear.

You might find the town lacking in ski resort atmosphere, and it's no great beauty; but it is lively and entertaining – particularly at weekends. It's completely Italian – this is Veneto, and the German language, widely used in next-door Süd Tirol, is nowhere to be seen or heard.

The place isn't at all exclusive – amid the boutiques is the most useful and diverting shop we've come across in a ski resort, the 4-storey Co-op department store, and 3-star hotels outnumber 4-star ones.

Convenience

It's not difficult to find apartments near one or other of the main lifts, less easy to find hotels. And wherever you stay you can't escape buses, taxis or driving if you want to cover the ground. Our inclination is to pick a good place near the centre, and accept the need to ride a bus every day. The bus services are efficient, but not simple; several go around the one-way ring road to serve the Faloria lift, but only #8 goes to the Tofana/Ra Valles lift and #9 to Socrepes.

Lodgings

Many of Cortina's affluent visitors are actually second-home owners, and the hotel scene is not particularly upscale – yes, there are four 5-star palaces (all but one well outside the town), but there are twice as many 3-star places as 4-star ones, and there's a handful of 2-stars.

The 4-star Poste is a classic traditional hotel on the central Corso. The equally central 2-star Montana gets good reports; B&B only. We've stayed happily in a very simple, good-value 3-star B&B place just over the ring road at the south end of the Corso, the Villa Neve. We've also enjoyed staying at the smoother 3-star Menardi, north of the town and a bearable walk from the Tofana/Ra Valles lift.

Out of the ordinary

About 20 of the mountain restaurants, across all sectors of the skiing – including most of the restaurants we recommend – are rifugios with rooms. Some are reachable by car, but Lagazuoi, at over 2700m, is certainly not. It's pretty simple, but also pretty memorable.

Bars and restaurants

There is some ski-booted life at the bottom of Socrepes at teatime, but après-ski mainly takes the cooler Italian form: dress up, head out for a little shopping and a coffee and cake or an aperitivo before dinner. There are some regular bars such as Janbo (with disco/karaoke), but the Cortina speciality is quieter wine bars, mostly with free antipasti. Enoteca Cortina is an institution – a fine old place with vaulted and panelled rooms; the Suite and Villa Sandi are cool little bars, the latter also operating as a restaurant. LP 26 is a bar/restaurant specialising in prosciutto. Baita Fraina does an exceptional range of wines by the glass.

Not surprisingly, there are some serious restaurants, mostly outside the centre. As we write in 2019, Tivoli, near the Socrepes slopes, retains its one Michelin star.

There are plenty of simpler places to eat. We had a surprisingly good meal at the busy, unpretentious 5 Torri in the centre, and good pizza at the lively Ponte at the south-east end of the Corso, on the ring road. We also liked the look of the Vizietto, but couldn't get a table.

In season, the several discos liven up at about the time we're heading for bed.

Off the slopes

There's quite a bit to do off the slopes, although there is at present nothing resembling a public aquatic centre/spa (there are of course plenty of hotels with pools and spas). A centre is being constructed on the north fringes of the town, to be ready for the world championships in 2021. The visuals look fab, with a six-lane 25m pool, extensive solarium and outdoor infinity pool.

There are no lift-served toboggan runs, either. But you can use the slopes of the defunct Mietres ski area, and several mountain restaurants will organise snowmobiles to get you up the mountain for a long run down – Rifugio Dibona and Malga Ra Stua both have groomed runs.

About 6km north of town at Fiames is an impressive array of cross-country skiing trails, at all levels, including a long trail following the disused railway line to the north, towards Dobbiaco. There are also difficult trails up at Passo Tre Croci, east of the town. There are lots (really, lots) of snowshoe routes, but footpaths seem to be confined to the toboggan runs mentioned above, which sounds scary.

The 60m ice rink built for the 1956 Olympics is now under an impressive roof; in 2026 it will be used for the curling events. It's used for competitions, including hockey matches, but is also open to the public for skating.

Near the ice rink is a planetarium. You can combine a show here with a visit to the observatory up at Col Drusciè, and dinner at the restaurant there.

If your plastic is in good shape, you could have a wonderful time shopping here. But don't overlook the Co-op.

For families

There are snow gardens at Socrepes and at the top of the Faloria cable car, but the towny resort with very little slope-side lodgings isn't an easy place to recommend for children.

It's not a conventional ski resort, from any point of view; this is Via Roma, around which life revolves

Courmayeur

In objective terms, Courmayeur doesn't really deserve a chapter in these pages: its ski area is just too small. And it's not perfectly formed, either – the mountain suits exactly the kind of skier who will find its size a problem.

But the resort has an established place in the British ski market, probably because the village is exceptionally captivating – at its core is a narrow pedestrian street lined by ancient stone buildings housing lively bars, tempting food shops, smooth boutiques and welcoming restaurants.

A small resort can make sense for a short break – but Courmayeur attracts weekend crowds from Turin and Milan, so make it a midweek one. Courmayeur can also offer an escape from bad weather in Chamonix, via the Mont Blanc tunnel. We've been glad of this option more than once.

The mountains in brief

Size The smallest ski area to get a chapter in these pages

Slopes An intermediate's mountain, partly wooded, partly open

Snow Modest altitude but good snow record and good snowmaking

System, Lift Good enough, although there are irritations

Sustenance Plenty of good spots with table service

For beginners We can't recommend it

For true blue skiers We can't recommend it

For the confident Excellent skiing, within the obvious size constraints

For experts A great range of off-piste routes in all directions

Fancy stuff The park looks OK to our inexpert eye

Courmayeur – the resort in brief

Convenience You'll probably be using buses, and riding a lift down

Lodgings Something for everyone, including the budget-conscious

Bars and restaurants A wide choice, with some great traditional bars

Off the slopes Quite a bit to do, but no swimming or tobogganing

For families Not an obvious candidate for a family trip

Pass notes	Key facts		Key ratings	
A six-day pass covers two days on the Mont Blanc lifts or any other resort in the Aosta valley. A full valley pass is available. The Mont Blanc Unlimited pass covers Chamonix, Megève and Verbier. Beginners can pay by the day to use the valley carpet-lift, or buy a lift pass to go higher.	Altitude	1225m	Size	✳
	Range	1210–2755m	Snow	✳✳✳✳
	Slopes (see text)	42km	Fast lifts	✳✳✳
	Where to stay, ideally		Mountain rest's	✳✳✳✳
	A stroll from the cable car to Plan Chécrouit.		Beginner	✳
			True blue	✳
	Websites		Confident	✳✳✳✳
	courmayeurmontblanc.it courmayeur-montblanc.com		Expert	✳✳✳✳
			Convenience	✳✳
			Families	✳✳
			Village charm	✳✳✳✳

The mountains in detail

In essence it's a simple mountain – the skiing is on the two flanks of a ridge, roughly represented by the blue and buff tints on the novel piste map shown opposite – but navigation is tricky in places where they meet.

The starting point for most people is the mid-mountain micro-resort of Plan Chécrouit, reached by a cross-valley cable car from the south end of the village, or by gondola from the suburb of Dolonne, across the river. For those driving to the lifts, the better option is the cable car to Pré de Pascal, at the opposite end of the ski area, from a point near Entrèves, below the Mont Blanc tunnel entrance. Nearby, an impressive modern cable car goes to Punta Helbronner at the shoulder of Mont Blanc, for off-piste runs back down and the famous Vallée Blanche to Chamonix (return by bus or taxi).

There are lift passes covering Chamonix or other Valle d'Aosta resorts, and bus services to get you there. La Thuile is 30 minutes away.

Size

We pestered Courmayeur for decades to come clean about the extent of its pistes, which were claimed to amount to 100km. Eventually the resort conceded that most of the 100km was actually off-piste routes. These days it claims 42km. But it also says the longest piste, from the top to Dolonne, is 7.4km; we make it 5.8km, which leaves us wondering if the real total is not 42km but more like 33km. Whatever: it rates ✳ for size, anyway.

Slopes

It's a mountain of two halves. Above Plan Chécrouit are sunny slopes that are mostly open; on the back of the hill in Val Veny are shady slopes, almost all in trees. Both flanks of the hill are quite steep, with blue runs taking roundabout routes to avoid the fall line. Take care on the red Bertolini in icy conditions – if you slide off to the left you can be in deep trouble.

As noted earlier, the longest run is close to 6km, with a vertical drop of

Although it's small, there are quite complex links between the two distinct sectors; Val Veny to the right

1400m from Cresta Youla, but this is exceptional – and the bottom part is not reliably open. You're more often skiing individual lifts from 900m to 1.5km long, rarely skiing verticals more than the 800m from the Gabba chair to Zerotta.

Snow

The slopes don't go very high, and those on the front face of the area get quite a bit of sun. But the snowfall record is good, despite the resort's location on the 'wrong' side of Mont Blanc, and snowmaking is extensive – we've enjoyed excellent piste skiing here during an early-season drought. All in all, you can expect good conditions.

System, Lift

Although there are some slow lifts, the key lifts are all fast. On weekdays the system can cope with demand, but on sunny spring weekends when there is an invasion from Turin problems can arise, particularly down at Zerotta, where the fast quad chair struggles.

The small Cresta Youla cable car shifts a miserable 350 people an hour; the red run it serves is worth doing now and again, but it's worth going early or late to avoid the queues. To our knowledge, the tiny top cable car to Cresta d'Arp (it holds just 15 people) has always served only off-piste runs, but in 2018 a black piste appeared on the piste map, adding 135m vertical to the run down to Col Chécrouit.

There's talk of replacing both of these top cable cars with a gondola. Don't hold your breath.

Sustenance

For a small area there are plenty of restaurants, including some notable ones.

You have a wide choice at or near Plan Chécrouit. The more relaxed downstairs restaurant of the Christiania is excellent. The new 5-star hotel, Le Massif, has a smooth outpost here, La Loge du Massif. Just above Plan, the Chaumière has a 'gourmet' restaurant downstairs, a simpler bistro upstairs. Slightly below Plan are two lovely old chalets doing great food – Chateau Branlant (head for the upstairs balcony if you can) and Chiecco. But be warned: the forceful Anna who runs rules Chiecco can be a bit temperamental, not to say bossy.

Up the hill, the cosy, rustic Maison

Vieille is an old favourite. On the back of the hill are several options, including a cluster around Zerotta; one reader strongly tips Capitan des Alpes.

More on the slopes

For beginners

The arrangements for beginners are far from ideal. There's a carpet-lift at Dolonne, paid for by the day, but it can lack snow. There's one up the cable car at Plan Chécrouit, but only for ski school pupils, we're told. Then there's one at Pré de Pascal, at the top of the cable car from Entrèves. The latter two require a lift pass, naturally. The real problem is that progression to longer runs is not easy – read the following section. Go elsewhere.

For true blue skiers

At Plan Chécrouit, the blue Pra Neyron run winding down from the ridge is your main option. This isn't the easiest of blues, with a steepish start, and it gets very busy, not least with school classes; it's also very sunny, and the snow suffers. Over the hill, there are long blues from both Pra Neyron and Pré de Pascal. These are gentler but narrow, and not so gentle as to make braking unnecessary – run 9 is especially narrow.

We don't think any of the true blue

skiers of our acquaintance would enjoy these blue runs. Go elsewhere.

For confident intermediates

Putting aside the area's limited extent, this is a mountain well suited to confident red run skiers. Gabba, Bertolini, Pra Neyron and Aretù are all fast chairs serving worthwhile red pistes. Then you've got the main Chécrouit gondola with 550m vertical, the run down to Dolonne served by a gondola, and the occasional excursion up the Youla cable car for a good but short 360m vertical descent on the best snow in the area.

And you've got the blacks in Val Veny to tackle, mostly not seriously steep and mostly shady, giving the hope of good snow conditions. Start with Rocce Bianche – not much steeper than nearby reds.

For experts

The blacks in Val Veny are mostly not serious, though most are definitely black. Diretta ends with a proper steep pitch. We're told Pista dell'Orso is never groomed, which is very unusual in Italy.

The short new black run at Cresta d'Arp starts gently then plunges right to join the main Lazey run, briefly becoming seriously steep and narrow; one source

puts it at 40°. A red option avoids that bit.

All of which won't amuse you for long. But there is a vast amount to do off-piste, including some epic stuff. The piste map shows two routes from Cresta d'Arp, but there are countless options, and quite a few from lower Youla, too. Some go to the Gabba chair, others down into Val Veny, others to Dolonne via the Dolonne couloir (to skier's right of the main Chécrouit slopes) or the wide Arp valley, right of that; one goes to La Balme near La Thuile.

The Skyway cable car on Mont Blanc rises over 2100m in two stages to Punta Helbronner, accessing multiple routes from the mid-station as well as long descents across the Toula glacier from the top. Or you can join the famous Vallée Blanche to Chamonix, neatly avoiding the notoriously scary ridge walk from the Aiguille du Midi on the French side.

If all of that seems a bit pedestrian, you can get heli-lifts to access routes on the Mont Blanc massif and elsewhere.

Fancy stuff

There is a fair-sized snow park, said to cater for everyone from novice to expert, between the Chécrouit and Aretù pistes above Plan Chécrouit. It includes a big air bag.

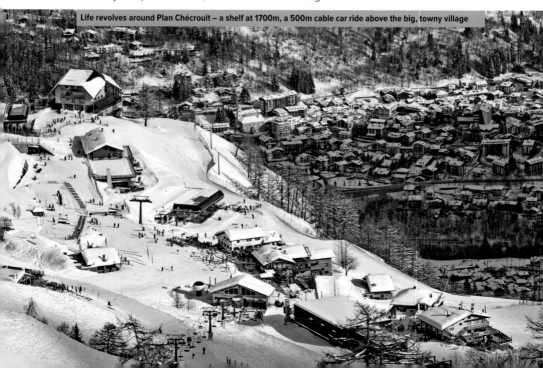

Life revolves around Plan Chécrouit – a shelf at 1700m, a 500m cable car ride above the big, towny village

Courmayeur – the resort

Although it spreads widely into pleasantly woody suburbs (scarred in places by apartment blocks), the essence of Courmayeur is the car-free Via Roma – a narrow, irregular, 300m-long street lined by old stone houses now accommodating designer boutiques, hotels, restaurants, welcoming bars and tempting food shops. On Friday evenings, the fur coats arrive in numbers from Turin for the passeggiata, revealing the resort to be one of Italy's most fashionable.

Convenience

The cable car is just over 300m from the south end of the focal Via Roma, so it's not difficult to find lodgings within walking distance of both. Buses link the village and the two lift bases, but they are not super-frequent. Some hotels run shuttles.

Lodgings

The hotel scene is dominated by 3-star places, but there are plenty of 2-stars and 4-stars, and now three 5-stars with the opening in 2018 of Le Massif. In the central Via Roma is the 2-star Cristallo, once a catered chalet hotel. For proximity to the cable car, look at the 3-star Triolet or the 4-star Pavillon. Less well placed but very well liked is the 3-star B&B Bouton d'Or. We also like the look of the charmingly woody 4-star Svizzero.

Bars and restaurants

These days the cable car runs through the evening, opening up the options of a beer on the mountain at close of play and of going up later for dinner. Via Roma has a parade of lively bars, most serving free antipasti – the Roma, the Privé and the back room of the Caffè della Posta are old favourites of ours. Try the American and Bar delle Guide, too.

There's lots of choice for dinner. Regular haunts of ours include the smart Cadran Solaire in Via Roma, La Terrazza at the north end, and the tiny Pizzeria du Tunnel. A short walk up from the village, Chalet Plan Gorret gets rave reviews.

With the cable car running in the evenings, you can now dine on the mountain, either at Plan Chécrouit or further up at Maison Vieille, reached by snowmobile.

Off the slopes

The big sports centre at Dolonne has a hockey-size ice rink, climbing wall, lots of other sports and spa facilities – but no pools. Five minutes down the valley is the thermal spa at Pré St Didier, with indoor/outdoor pools – but reports suggest it gets very crowded. At the north end of the village is an Alpine museum. There are 20km of cross-country trails in Val Ferret, at the foot of Mont Blanc. There are snowshoe routes there, and in Val Veny and up on the mountain. We've seen no mention of toboggans.

It's worth riding the two-stage cable car (with rotating cabins) to Punta Helbronner (3466m) just for the views.

For families

This doesn't strike us as an obvious choice for a holiday with young children, even though there are the necessary facilities. There are countless better spots.

Espace San Bernardo

La Thuile + La Rosière (France)

The Colle del Piccolo San Bernado, to use the Sunday name, is a pass between the French Tarentaise and Italian Aosta valleys – not an especially high pass, but closed in winter. La Thuile is at the foot of the climb from Italy; La Rosière is quite close to the pass, on the French side.

The two resorts are linked by lifts and pistes over the pass, forming a fair-sized ski area. La Thuile's half of the skiing is varied and interesting, and is blessed (even more than most Italian resorts) with the special merit of a blissful lack of crowds (on weekdays, at least) even in high season.

La Thuile is based on a restored mining village; it's pleasant but dull, and a cheaper base for the area than La Rosière.

The mountains in brief

Size Mid-sized, including La Rosière, but with plenty of variety

Slopes Local slopes offer an interesting mix of everything

Snow Good snowfall record, and most slopes are quite high and shady

System, Lift Key lifts are fast and queues rare except on peak weekends

Sustenance Some decent places – a much better choice than in La Rosière

For beginners Good slopes, and a sensible range of payment deals

For true blue skiers Good slopes, but limited extent; La Rosière is tricky

For the confident An interesting area, though many red runs are very tame

For experts Quite a lot to do, including some excellent off-piste routes

Fancy stuff No proper park now – just a funslope

La Thuile – the resort in brief

Convenience Some lodgings at the base, but most people need the bus

Lodgings Mainly simple places, but a full range is available

Bars and restaurants A quiet village, but some good spots

Off the slopes Not a great range of options; good snowshoe trails, though

For families Stay at the lift base and you should have fun

Pass notes	Key facts		Key ratings	
The six-day pass covers two days in other Aosta valley resorts (eg Cervinia and Courmayeur). A full valley pass is available. Beginners can buy day passes for the village carpet-lift, or for that plus the village chair-lift, or for those plus the gondola and the Combe chair-lift at the top of it.	Altitude	1450m	Size	★★★
	Range	1470–2800m	Snow	★★★★
	Slopes (see text)	152km	Fast lifts	★★★★
			Mountain rest's	★★★
	Where to stay, ideally		Beginner	★★★
	It's a question of priorities.		True blue	★★★
			Confident	★★★★
	Websites		Expert	★★★
	lathuile.it		Convenience	★★★
			Families	★★★
			Village charm	★★★

The mountains in detail

There is skiing at village level, but in practice for most visitors the base of the ski area is up the hill at Les Suches. From there, chair-lifts go up to Chaz Dura and Col de Fourclaz, on the ridge that separates the gentle home slopes from more challenging slopes above the pass. Pistes link across the mountainside to a slightly separate area of runs served mainly by the Argillien fast chair.

A red run from Chaz Dura goes down to a chair-lift on the pass side of the minor peak of Belvedere, from which point a blue run goes down to the Chardonnet chair that forms the link with French La Rosière.

From Les Suches and from various points on the top ridge there are runs to the village, through or skirting the dense forest.

Size

In 2018, to celebrate the expansion of La Rosière's skiing by the building of new lifts on Mont Valaisan, these resorts joined the small band of ski areas to have the extent of their pistes certified by the estimable Christoph Schrahe. The result was 152km, bang in the middle of our ✳✳✳ category. We're told this total is divided about equally between France and Italy; we'd have guessed Italy has a bit more than half – and totting up the lengths of individual runs on La Thuile's website gives a figure of 92km.

Slopes

It's the kind of mountain that's more common in the Tirol than in Italy – steep wooded slopes immediately above the village, with much gentler open slopes above the trees. From Belvedere at the top of the La Thuile slopes to the village is a vertical drop of almost 1150m, and you can ski that in several ways, including runs at the extremities of the area – about 11km long in each case. Of course, those runs are exceptional; the Fourclaz chair-lift on the slopes above the pass, where keen skiers might do laps, gives 475m.

The lovely, long, away-from-the-lifts run on skier's right of the area – this top part could be classified blue

Snow

La Thuile's snowfall record isn't as good as that of La Rosière (particularly at village level – La Rosière is 400m higher) but it's pretty good. The slopes are not excessively sunny, and most of the time you're skiing at a decent altitude, above 2000m. There is snowmaking on 40km of La Thuile's local pistes.

System, Lift

There's a powerful gondola from the base (with a fast chair in parallel) and most of the key lifts are fast chairs – most slow lifts can be avoided (those around the French link constituting an exception). The lift system seems to cope, even on sunny weekends when there is the usual invasion from Turin and Milan; on weekdays, we have never seen a queue of any kind, even in February.

Sustenance

There are quite a few restaurants – identified by letters on the map, for once – but the lunch situation isn't great by Italian standards, though it's way better than over the hill in La Rosière. We have a love-hate relationship with Maison Carrel, having had very good and very disappointing experiences – and most recently a mixed one. We also like the eccentrically decorated Off Shore, not least for its nostalgic music. The Ratrak is fine if it's not bursting with kids. Baita le Foyer is strongly tipped by readers, as is the newish Petit Skieur on the nursery slopes. Nearby, hardly a mountain restaurant but on the very edge of the village, the Tatà takes a lot of beating.

More on the slopes

For beginners

There are three carpet-lifts at village level – two short free ones and a not-free one 100m long – and a 50m one at Les Suches. At village level your next step is the Maison Blanche chair-lift, serving a gentle winding blue back to the base. Or the gondola up to Les Suches to ski the

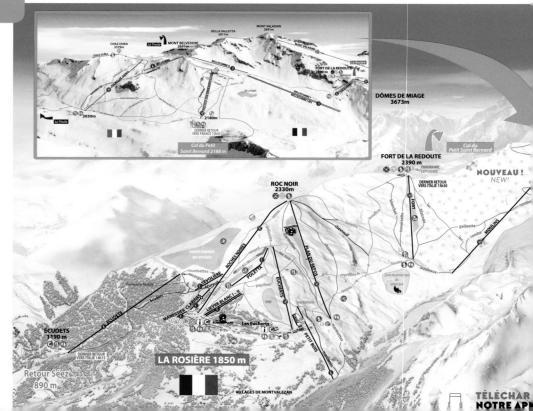

ROC NOIR
2330m

FORT DE LA REDOUTE
2390 m

DÔMES DE MIAGE
3673m

NOUVEAU !
NEW!

LA ROSIÈRE 1850 m

Retour Séez
890 m

ECUDETS
1190 m

VILLAGES DE MONTVALEZAN

TÉLÉCHAR
NOTRE API

longer blues served by the Combe chair-lift – read the next section.

The lift pass arrangements are well thought out, allowing you to choose what you want access to. Well done, La Thuile.

For true blue skiers

Above Les Suches is a row of easy blue runs, served by the Combe slow chair starting near the top gondola station and the Chalet fast chair-lift starting slightly lower. The runs that more or less follow the lift lines – Terres Noires and Boulevard – are slightly more challenging than the others. And above them is more of the same served by the Gran Testa drag-lift, giving a run of about a mile down to Les Suches.

The red runs to skier's right of the blues, on the Argillien chair, are largely of blue gradient, too – but they are red because they get appreciably steeper towards the lift base. Leysé has probably the easiest approach. The runs to the Arnouvaz chair, the ones from Col de Fourclaz at the top of the area and the

ones above the pass are genuine reds.

So there isn't a huge amount to do, especially if the reds on the Argillien chair are too much for you. But read the feature panel on the link with La Rosière.

For confident intermediates

It's an interesting area for a competent skier, but there is less red-run skiing than the map suggests – on the front of the area, much of the red skiing on the upper slopes could be classified blue, and it's only at the top and towards the bottom that there are genuine red stretches. The runs on the back of the ridge, down to the pass, are more challenging, genuine reds; and the blacks there are worth a look – try Touriasse and the middle section of Belvedere first.

The long, scenic, away-from-the-lifts red 18 on skier's right of the whole area is a splendid, easy run, but red 6 beyond the Arnouvaz chair often has poor snow – it may be icy and therefore quite difficult ('a gnarly nightmare' for one reader) or it may be closed. The similarly scenic run

7 follows the gentle pass road; it drops only 600m vertical in its 11km, so turns are rarely needed – but heavy snow can mean poling to keep moving.

The red run 4 from Les Suches to the village is a good way to get home – at first an easy traverse into the woods, but then some proper red skiing before joining run 7, mentioned above.

The new red runs opened in 2018 on Mont Valaisan at La Rosière opened after *Where to Ski in France* was published, but we were able to try them in 2019. Lac (49) to reach the new lifts is a fine red cruise, but we're less convinced by the runs on the lifts: the top red run (53, called 2800) is a narrow track for most of its length – and tends to get worn and icy, we're told. Combe (52) on the lower chair is a bit wider but has pitches verging on black gradient in the middle – fine for strong, confident intermediates, not for others.

For experts

There are worthwhile black runs in two main areas. Those over the ridge above the pass are rightly black, but steep only in places. The ones heading through the woods to the village offer more sustained challenges. The highest of the three ways into the Franco Berthod run, in particular,

is seriously steep (36°, they say). Muret, on skier's right of the lifts, is a fine run, pleasantly quiet, reaching proper black steepness in stretches; it involves skiing the last mile of red run 6.

The off-piste potential is considerable. There are good runs from Chaz Dura (and points on the ridge either side of the peak) towards the pass road, ranging from shady to sunny, including the well known Direttissima. Those to skier's right of the peak go down to join or cross piste 4. Belvedere has a row of stiff but short descents on its north face – in the past there was a very steep piste here, abandoned we guess because of avalanche problems.

By hiking along the French border ridge you can reach gloriously long runs from the shoulder of Bella Valletta, going north-east towards La Thuile.

There are some excellent runs reached via La Rosière's new Mont Valaisan lift and from the peak a 90m 20-minute hike up. Some go into Italy to join the Bella Valletta runs, others north-west, staying in France – and the bowl to skier's left of the lifts offers huge amounts of terrain above La Rosière.

Back at La Thuile, for bad-weather days there are runs in the trees above the

There's genuinely steep skiing in the woods leading down to the nursery slope, beyond the Planibel complex

village. The lightly wooded slopes to left and right of the Muret black piste are the obvious target if you like a bit of space between the trees, but there are also good routes dropping off red piste 4 that are not too tight.

Heli-drops are allowed in Valle d'Aosta. The Rutor glacier is a favourite – return to La Rosière by taxi to ride the lifts home.

Fancy stuff

The resort abandoned its Wazimu snow park at Les Suches in 2017. But now, amid the blue slopes is the more family-oriented Fun Slope LTH.

At the pass is an area dedicated to snowkiting; tuition is available, and there's a special day pass covering just the lifts you need to get up to the pass.

The French connection – La Rosière

You'll probably be buying a lift pass that covers La Rosière as well as La Thuile, so if you're a keen skier, an outing to France (or two) is a no-brainer.

It takes three chair-lift rides to get to the border, then a fourth to get to the top of the French slopes. You can take the slow Belvedere chair to reach the slow chair that completes the link, or ski on past it to the fast Piccolo San Bernardo chair. On the way back you have to take a mile-long drag-lift; then you can go on to take the slightly shorter drag above it, or ski down to the Fourclaz chair.

The link also involves skiing red runs, in both directions. Neither is seriously steep, but a true blue skier will want to approach with caution, and perhaps take advice on the snow conditions. Outward, from the ridge above La Thuile, piste 7 takes a dog-leg track to skier's right which is a reasonable gradient but quite narrow.

The return run, shown in the photo below, is a bigger challenge – steep in parts, narrow in others; it's probably too much for many true blue skiers. You could always ski down to the chair and check it out before making your call; but bear in mind that you'll probably be skiing it late in the day, when it won't be at its easiest.

The French pistes are generally busier (beware high-season weeks when French and British school holidays coincide, in particular), and although La Rosière gets a lot of snow it also gets a lot of sun, so after midwinter you may find the snow hard or heavy, or that it gets bumped up.

Perhaps a more important weakness is that the lunch opportunities are not great – only the Antigel, on the home slope just above the village, is easy to recommend. Prices are higher than in Italy, too.

Be aware that wind or heavy snow can close the link, sometimes for days.

The linking run back from La Rosière is easier than it once was, but is still properly classified red

La Thuile – the resort

La Thuile is a curious resort. Its mining-village centre has been thoroughly restored, but most of the lodgings are well away from there, leaving it rather lifeless. And the separate lift base area – about 700m from the middle of the old village – is dominated by large apartment buildings. But there other areas of development spread around the spacious valley that are quite pleasantly rustic.

Convenience

It all depends where you stay. There are lodgings at the lift base, but many of the more attractive places are elsewhere – between the nursery slopes and the road up to the pass, or across the river from the lift base. There are ski-buses circulating, and the better hotels have their own shuttles.

Lodgings

There's a good range of options, whether you want a hotel or an apartment.

Simple places dominate, but on our last visit we stayed very happily at the 5-star Montana Lodge, which feels a bit out of place in this glitz-free resort. Good staff, spacious modern rooms, fab pool and a seriously good restaurant. It's over the river, a walkable distance from the lifts, but there is an on-call shuttle.

There are several 4-star places, and we have enjoyed staying at the 4-star Miramonti, across the river from the old village – smartly renovated, good food, shuttle to the lifts.

For convenience, you won't beat the 4-star TH La Thuile-Planibel, as the big hotel/apartment complex at the lift base now wants to be called. But we'd go for the much more personal 3-star hotel Boton d'Or, a short walk away.

Bars and restaurants

This isn't a place for on-mountain après, but at the base the Cage aux Folles is pleasantly popular. Angela's Cafe is inconveniently set at the north end of the village, but is noted for its variety of hot chocolate. Both do free antipasti.

For dinner, the Tatà is a well-run place in a lovely rustic building, next to the nursery slopes. Maison Laurent and Coppapan are also recommended by readers.

Off the slopes

Snowshoe walking is big around here, with eight recognised trails along the quiet valleys south-east and north-east of the village. On the big open area east of the village are several cross-country trails, including a red one 7km long. There are further trails, blue, red and black, a few km away at Arpy. Both the Planibel and Montana hotel swimming pools are open to the public. Half an hour's drive away in the main Aosta valley is the thermal spa at Pré St Didier, with indoor/outdoor pools – but reports suggest it gets very crowded. Sadly, we are told there is no organised tobogganing.

For families

The lift base area roughly resembles the French resort of Flaine, famously good for small children, and staying at the Planibel complex should work very well; acres of snow to play on.

Kronplatz – San Vigilio

San Vigilio / Bruneck

Forgive the lingo mash-up: this is a confusing region (the local language is actually Ladin). We're using the names that seem most commonly used.

Kronplatz is an extraordinary mountain – an isolated dome draped with an absurd number of gondolas, offering some easy skiing at altitude but also long, challenging top-to-bottom runs to lift stations around the town of Bruneck to the north. It's a classic weekend resort; staying for a week, you'd be wanting to take trips elsewhere (easily done, by train or bus).

Our preferred base, San Vigilio, is extraordinary, too – an attractive, prosperous village, widely spread but consisting more of open fields than of buildings. It has its own small sector of slopes west of the village.

The mountains in brief

Size On the small side, but outings to other areas are possible

Slopes From gentle and open at the top, to steeper and wooded low down

Snow 100% snowmaking means you can normally be confident

System, Lift Powerful and comfortable; but removing skis becomes a drag

Sustenance Plenty of choice, and some good table-service places

For beginners The village gondolas serve excellent easy blue runs

For true blue skiers A fair bit to do, but less than the map suggests

For the confident Some cracking runs, but not many of them

For experts For once, the pistes are the thing – the famous five blacks

Fancy stuff The park looks OK, with a choice of lifts

San Vigilio – the resort in brief

Convenience Most people need the village buses – but not all

Lodgings Something for everyone, including the budget-conscious

Bars and restaurants It's a quiet place, but there are places to go

Off the slopes Walking, sledging, skating – but no public pool

For families An attractive prospect – a quiet village with some easy slopes

Pass notes	Key facts		Key ratings	
There's a local pass saving a few euros on the cost of the Dolomiti Superski pass which would cover outings to Alta Badia or Drei Zinnen. Beginners can buy points cards.	Altitude	1200m	Size	**
	Range	950–2275m	Snow	****
	Slopes (see text)	78km	Fast lifts	*****
	Where to stay, ideally		Mountain rest's	****
	Close to one or other of the two access gondolas.		Beginner	****
			True blue	***
	Websites		Confident	****
	kronplatz.com		Expert	***
	sanvigilio.com		Convenience	***
	pustertal.org		Families	****
			Village charm	****

The mountains in detail

The main lift base, with two mid-capacity gondolas and huge areas of parking, is on the north side of the conical mountain at Reischach, 2.5km from central Bruneck. To looker's left, a very long and more powerful gondola goes up from a railway station at Percha. Left again, on the east side is a smaller lift base at Gassl, an outpost of Olang, with two mid-capacity gondolas. These latter two lift bases have the advantage for many skiers of red runs to the bottom; Reischach has only two black runs.

From San Vigilio, the Miara gondola takes you to (or almost to) the col of Passo Furcia, where there are short lifts and runs on the lower slopes of Piz da Peres and the powerful Ruis gondola goes on up to Kronplatz.

The map suggests that the Ruis gondola and its slopes are just to the right of the Bruneck slopes, separated only by a narrow strip of forest, but actually they are on the diametrically opposite south side of the hill.

The lift system is extraordinary. It's not a big area, but for the 2020 season it has an absurd 22 gondolas – and 4 fast chair-lifts (no slow ones).

On the opposite side of San Vigilio, linked by a short cross-village gondola, is a small area of slopes below Piz de Plaies, accessed by the Pedagà gondola. From a valley lift station on the back of this hill, buses run to Alta Badia. From Percha, trains run to the Drei Zinnen area.

Size

Kronplatz seems to have got into a tangle with its run lengths. It claims widely a total of 119km, and its website lists lengths for individual runs that add up to exactly that. It also explains how these lengths are arrived at – by a bizarre method. They take the area of snow the lift company grooms and divide that by an average piste width of 40m. The result is piste lengths exaggerated, we reckon, by as much as 70% or even 80%.

Ah, but then we find that the 2019-20 piste map includes a list of piste lengths that look much more sensible. They add up to 78km, a total which, by amazing coincidence, matches almost exactly the most recent figure for the area published by Christoph Schrahe. So, 78km it is and, like so many Italian resorts, Kronplatz gets a ✹✹ size rating as a result.

The 20-minute bus service from Piculin to Alta Badia opens up huge amounts of additional skiing – and San Vigilio is a good starting point. Bear in mind that you are deposited by the bus on the fringe of Alta Badia. San Vigilio is not nearly such a good starting point for the Ski Pusteral Express trains to the Drei Zinnen area from the Percha lift base; the trains take about 40 minutes.

Slopes

The summit area has easy open slopes going east and south, steeper slopes going north. Most of the mountain, below about 2000m, is wooded.

A key feature is the long top-to-bottom runs. The two black runs to Reischach are about 5km long, with verticals of almost 1300m. If you include the blue run above it, the Ried red run to Percha has much the same vertical but is 7km long. The home run to San Vigilio is interrupted by a lift ride, but adds up to about 6km.

When snow or crowds make descents to the valley station rubbish, you'll be riding upper lifts with modest verticals – 200m to 400m, sometimes 500m.

Snow

The area's snowfall record is not great, and it relies heavily on snowmaking, which covers all the pistes. (They say the resort was the first in Europe to adopt it.) So, as elsewhere in this part of the world, a drought is not a problem.

System, Lift

What can we say? The lift system is amazing. The last slow chair-lift was replaced in 2019 by yet another powerful gondola. What we can say, of course, is that Kronplatz hasn't built 26 fast, powerful lifts for nothing – it has built them to be filled. At the summit, eight of these lifts meet, with the ability to deliver 1,000 people every 3 minutes, or less. On a peak weekend day the result, to quote a well-travelled observer of these things, is 'horrible, like Piccadilly Circus on a busy day – the black pistes are crowded, the blue pistes ridiculously so'. Of course, bad-weather off-peak weekdays are different.

A real drawback of the preponderance of gondolas is the need to be forever removing your skis to take a lift. Another irritation is that you usually have to change lifts at gondola mid-stations.

Sustenance

There are lots of mountain restaurants, marked but not named on the piste map.

At the summit, we sadly missed the chance to renew acquaintance with the food of star local chef Norbert Niederkofler (from the St Hubertus restaurant in San Cassiano) who directs things at the Alpinn, an extraordinary panoramic room at the Lumen museum. For more routine meals at the top, Corones Hütte will do nicely.

On the way down to Olang, Oberegger Alm is too popular for its own good but does a very good job of keeping everyone happy while squeezed on to shared tables. The dumplings are famous, apparently. Just above it, Rifugio Lorenzi has a good reputation, too.

On the red piste from the summit towards Passo Furcia, Graziani Lodge is claimed to be the oldest hut on the mountain – and it is still in the same family after 130+ years. Across the pass on the Piz da Peres slopes, Ücia Picio Pré is a lovely little log-built chalet doing excellent food including Ladin dishes.

On the Piz de Plaies slopes, La Para on the red piste gets good reports.

More on the slopes

For beginners

In ski school, you may start on a carpet-lift in the village. If not, you start on the very short Cianross gondola to ski the easy, slightly less short Corn run. Then, cross the village to ride the much longer Miara gondola; this serves a lovely easy blue – wide, three times as long as the alternative Pedagà blue, and gentler.

For true blue skiers

There's a fair bit to do here, but less than you might think. For a start, the east-facing flank of the upper mountain, which has five blue pistes marked on the piste map, is more or less one vast, treeless, featureless slope.

Secondly, the map is distorted to exaggerate the length of some runs – Pracken, for example, looks like it goes almost to the bottom, but it actually ends above 1600m; Plateau looks like it goes well below mid-mountain, but it ends only 250m below the peak.

And thirdly, some of the lower blues may be too challenging for you. Once into the woods, the runs have a bit more character, but are also a bit steeper; Hinterberg (27) becomes quite challenging, for example. Beware Lorenzi (24): this is below the benign Plateau (6), but is much steeper, and in many resorts might be classified red.

On the way back to San Vigilio, Furcia 9 to Passo Furcia is no problem, but it's a shame that Col Toron below that is a red – not an especially steep one, but steep enough in its middle section to worry a true blue skier – so you're in for a gondola ride down. The blue on the lower mountain is fine, as explained above.

For confident intermediates

There are some excellent red runs, but they don't add up to a lot.

Basically, on the main mountain there are five descents of interest. There are rewarding but rather short ones to the north (Pramstall) and the south (Furcia 12), two adjacent ones to the east (Gassl and Arndt/World Record Piste – don't ask) which are longer and a bit steeper, and to the north-east the longest and most interesting, Ried; this can be combined with blue runs above it to make a top-to-bottom descent of around 7km.

From the top of the Piz da Peres slopes to the gondola mid-station on the home slope to San Vigilio is a descent of over 500m vertical, while the Piz de Plaies slopes offer rather less – 435m.

And what about the blacks? Well, as so often, it depends on the snow conditions. Read the following section.

For experts

Kronplatz makes quite a fuss about having five black runs, and with some justification – they are all genuine blacks, although they do of course vary. They are all groomed regularly.

The piste that attracts most attention is not on Kronplatz itself but is one of two

Kronplatz from the east, with just a few of its gondolas in view; San Vigilio is to the left, Bruneck to the right

shortish blacks on Piz de Plaies – Piculin, on the back of the hill. This is talked up as being exceptionally steep – up to 36° they say. We're sceptical about that, but it is steep, for sure, and can be extremely challenging because of snow conditions. The steep section at the top faces south-west, the ideal orientation to produce slush in the afternoon and ice in the morning; approach with caution. Erta on the front side is just as steep towards the end, but usually enjoys much better snow.

We're more taken by the two blacks that dominate the piste map, running from the top to Reischach at the bottom – both about 5km long with a vertical of almost 1300m. These are fabulous runs when in good shape (which usually means early in the day). As those statistics suggest (average gradient 26%, or about 15°) they contain long stretches of blue and red steepness and only short stretches of black steepness. Herrnegg is probably more challenging than Sylvester, with slightly steeper pitches.

Which leaves the Pre da Peres piste at Passo Furcia – a short run, black only for a short stretch in the middle.

Fancy stuff

Kronplatz's snow park is located on the open upper slopes between the Belvedere and Plateau pistes, on the left of the piste map. It's a fair size, featuring an easy line, a medium rail line and a medium kicker line, plus a family fun line.

Jib Park Korer is on the Korer piste, down at the Reischach valley station – primarily designed for kids, and open two evenings a week as well as daytime.

San Vigilio – the resort

San Vigilio di Marebbe is a traditional village enjoying a pretty wooded setting in a quiet dead-end valley, slightly elevated above the Pustertal to the north. The unusually spacious layout, with most of the development along lanes set around a dozen open fields, gives the place a rustic air.

Convenience

It depends where you stay. The village is about 2km long, with its two lift stations slightly to the north of the main areas of development. The cross-village gondola linking them is 400m long. There are plenty of lodgings within walking distance of one or both lift stations, and a few right at or above a station. But there are also plenty where you'll need to call on the hotel shuttle, or on the ski-buses that run on three routes around the village.

Lodgings

There's a wide choice of hotels, guest houses and small apartment residences. 3-star hotels outnumber 4-stars, just. We stayed very happily at the well run 4-star Excelsior Dolomites Life Resort, in a great ski-in/ski-out location above the Pedagà lift station.

Out of the ordinary

Some mountain restaurants have rooms. La Para, halfway down the local red run, has fine views over the village. Graziani Lodge, on the south slope of Kronplatz, lets four woody private chalets as well as rooms in the lodge. The 4-star Spaces hotel, just above the mid-station of the Miara gondola, is a rather different thing – a full-blown cutting-edge 'design' hotel.

In the village, the 3-star hotel Al Plan advertises 24 rooms, 17 Vespas, 35 classic cars and motorbikes (some available for hire) and 283 clocks: it's a museum as well as a hotel – and it's in an excellent position at the Miara lift base.

Bars and restaurants

It's a quiet village, but there is life in the Scodada bar by the Miara lift station at close of play. Later on the Busstop pub, complete with a bus half in and half out of the place, is busy until it closes at 2am. Meo Pizza Aperitivo is tipped for quiet drinks and good pizza.

There's an adequate choice of eateries, of which Fana Ladina has a fair claim to be the best; it serves Ladin specialities in wood-panelled rooms in one of the oldest houses in the village.

Off the slopes

An unusual feature of the mountain is that there are two museums at the top. One is part of a set of six devoted to mountains, mountain people and mountaineering, set up by the amazing mountaineer Reinhold Messner, born in Brixen, in Süd Tirol. In 1978 Messner and Peter Habeler were the first to climb Everest without the aid of oxygen tanks, and in 1980 Messner was the first to climb it solo. The museum, largely underground, was designed by the equally famous Zaha Hadid. The other museum is Lumen, devoted to mountain photography. Be aware: they close early.

The very short gondola at the bottom of the Piz de Plaies slopes serves a short but worthwhile toboggan run, not a common thing in Italian resorts. For more of an adventure, you can haul your sledge 3km up from the village of Rina, a few km north-west of San Vigilio, to the Munt da Rina restaurant, to descend the path. There's a floodlit natural ice rink close to the village centre. There's no public swimming pool.

There are long cross-country trails from the fringes of the village along the dead-end valley to the south-east, but also lots of other trails in the Pustertal region. There are footpaths along the valley too, but also more strenuous walks up into the ski slopes on the east side of Kronplatz. Snowshoe routes include some quite adventurous ones into the nearby nature reserve.

For families

The relaxed, rustic village should suit young families well. There are snow gardens near the Cianross gondola station in the village and at the Kronplatz summit area. On the Pedagà slope at S Vigilio is a kids' terrain park.

The Bruneck option

Although there is nothing resembling a ski resort, on the north side of the mountain there are plenty of lodgings in several locations – spread around the Reischach lift base, in the attractive historic town of Bruneck nearby and in various surrounding villages. At Reischach, you won't do better than the 3-star hotel Tannenhof, 400m from the lift station.

Austrian-style après-ski is abundantly present at the Reischach lift base, in the big, brash K1 bar/pizzeria/nightclub, the slightly more traditional Giggeralm and the hotel Heinz's Tenne bar. The Gassl at the Olang base is popular, too.

The 1km-long gondola at the Reischach base serves a snow park, an illuminated piste and a toboggan run. What an excellent device!

One of the six Messner museums mentioned above is in Bruneck.

It's an unusual village, developed around countless open fields; the piste from Kronplatz is visible top left

Madesimo

Two hours' drive north from central Milan, high up near the Swiss border, Madesimo makes a natural weekend retreat for the city's residents. For a week's holiday, the place is not so obviously appealing – the pistes are extremely limited, and there isn't a lot of anything else to do. But its slopes are gloriously quiet once the weekenders' bags are packed.

The resort is famous for a particular run, the Canalone. It is an excellent descent – steep, long and scenic. But it became famous when it was a black piste, and was among the most challenging. Now it is classified as off-piste – although the situation is blurred. Read on.

The village is pleasant, uncommercialised but plain, dominated by second homes and therefore, like the pistes, quiet except at weekends.

The mountains in brief

Size In terms of piste km, one of the smallest resorts in these pages

Slopes A mountainside of essentially red gradient, mostly wooded

Snow Altitude and orientation help

System, Lift Mostly fast lifts, but the cable car to the top gets huge queues

Sustenance Very limited choice, but you won't starve

For beginners Excellent nursery slopes; progression slopes not ideal

For true blue skiers Much less good than a glance at the map suggests

For the confident Some good runs, but not many of them

For experts Some good runs, but you're dependent on that cable car

Fancy stuff The park looks OK to our untrained eye

Madesimo – the resort in brief

Convenience Not a ski-in resort, but walks range from trivial to bearable

Lodgings Nothing swanky, but some good mid-market options

Bars and restaurants A quiet village, with a few good places

Off the slopes Great snowmobiling, and a sports centre with an ice rink

For families Stay near the snow and it should work well enough

Pass notes	Key facts		Key ratings	
As well as regular passes there are passes for five non-consecutive days. Beginners can buy cheap tickets for five rides on the two beginner chair-lifts.	Altitude	1540m	Size	✳
	Range	1540–2880m	Snow	✳✳✳
	Slopes (see text)	35km	Fast lifts	✳✳✳✳
	Where to stay, ideally		Mountain rest's	✳
	Near whichever lift base suits your purpose.		Beginner	✳✳✳
			True blue	✳✳
	Websites		Confident	✳✳✳✳
	madesimo.eu		Expert	✳✳✳
	skiareavalchiavenna.it madesimo.com (operated by Valchiavenna tourism consortium)		Convenience	✳✳✳✳
			Families	✳✳✳
			Village charm	✳✳✳

The mountains in detail

The main axis of the lift system is a chain of gondola/chair/cable car from the village centre to **Pizzo Groppera**. Off-piste routes are the only way back from the top, apart from another cable car ride. In Val di Lei on the back of the hill is a double chair. On looker's left of this axis, the skiing on the fast Montalto chair from the north end of the village is well linked.

To looker's right, though, a stream separates the slopes served by the Lago Azzurro fast chair – they are linked only at altitude. To the right again, the lifts at Motta can be reached by a long traverse or via higher lifts on what the piste map calls La Colmanetta, the high point of the piste skiing.

The hamlet of Motta is at the top of a quick underground funicular from the valley town of Campodolcino, where there are big car parks.

Size

We've seen claims of less than 50km for Madesimo's pistes, and claims of 60km. But the individual piste lengths helpfully provided on the printed piste map total only 35km, which feels nearer the mark. A dozen of the blue runs on the map are just links across the mountain, identified as 'skiwegs'. These add up to almost 6km, so you could say the worthwhile skiing amounts to less than 30km.

Anyway, it's clear that Madesimo merits only * and rivals Courmayeur for the smallest-area-in-the-book award.

Slopes

As the map suggests, the slopes directly above the village are entirely wooded, while the higher runs and the slopes above Motta are open – as are the runs on extreme skier's right of the area. It's essentially a red-run mountain, with the blues taking roundabout routes.

The draw for experts is the famous Canalone. In the distant past it was a black piste; it is now marked on the map, along with the Camosci variant and the longer Angeloga run, as off-piste. Signs at the cable car state that the runs are

The trees extend almost up to the lower cable car station, at Cima Sole; top gondola station in the foreground

'not marked, not classified, not patrolled nor protected'. In fact, Canalone at least is marked roughly, in the classic itinerary style. But the lift company has confirmed to us that the runs are simply off-piste – they are not closed because of avalanche risk, and require full avalanche kit.

The top of the Groppera lift (2880m) isn't quite as high as the map suggests. This still permits a descent of 1340m vertical, but most of that is on one of the off-piste routes. The top of the piste system on the front of the mountain is La Colmanetta, giving a run to the village of almost 700m vertical.

Snow

The snowfall here isn't great, but the altitudes are reasonable. The main slopes face north-west, so they don't get much afternoon sun. The Val di Lei slopes face north-east, so the sun isn't a problem there. There is snowmaking on about two-thirds of the area. The slopes above Motta are often affected by wind.

System, Lift

The system is a modern one, with fast chairs almost everywhere they're needed.

The clear exception is the high lifts on Pizzo Groppera. The cable car is small, long and quite slow by cable car standards, so it shifts only 360 people an hour. On a powder day, this is nowhere near enough. On a weekend powder day, its inadequacy is laughable. The Val di Lei double chair is also slow, of course.

The funicular to Motta can bring 3500 people an hour up from Campodolcino in the valley, and may do so on a fine Sunday, swamping the Motta chair.

Sustenance

You won't starve, but the mountain restaurants are not a highlight. The big Larici at the top of the gondola is the dominant place, and seems to satisfy customers despite its scale (550 seats inside, 800 on the terrace). Just down the piste, Acquarela is more personal but noisy. In a fine secluded spot over in Val di Lei is a small chalet with a big terrace.

More on the slopes

For beginners

The 350m-long Arlecchino quad chair serves a nice gentle slope at the north end of the village, with restaurants on hand for R&R. From there you can move on to riding the longer Montalto chair and skiing the Pianello blue run – not specially tough, but not the easiest of blues.

For true blue skiers

As we've explained, many of the blue runs that make the map look so appetising are just tracks designed to get you across the mountain from one place to another. In practice, there are just four worthwhile blue runs.

Pianello on the Montalto chair, on skier's right of the area, is a good blue – not the easiest, though. The rest of the skiing is reached via the Lago Azzurro chair at the south end of the village.

Serenissima on the Motta chair is a pleasant, easy run although quite short – 1km long. The run from the higher Serenissima chair, which starts as Cascèe and becomes Angiolezza, is longer and a bit more challenging. Much the longest (about 2.5km) and most satisfying is Lago Azzurro, which goes through the forest from the eponymous chair; unfortunately, the final short pitch to the village lift station is steep – check it out from the bottom before you ride the chair.

For confident intermediates

There's more for a competent skier to do. Practically all the red pistes deserve the classification, although some are on the soft side. The runs on the lower mountain – lower Vanoni, Interpista, lower Valsecchi – start out a bit tame but steepen as they approach the village. Add in the upper sections from Cima Sole and Colmanetta, though, and you have quite long and satisfying descents – Valsecchi (17) in particular. It's worth getting over to Val di Lei at times when the Groppera cable car is not rammed – nicely varied reds (although fewer than in the past) and time to relax on the slow chair-lift.

And then you have the black pistes. Pedroncelli on the Montalto chair starts steeply but really is just a tough red run. Interpista from Cima Sole is a genuine black, but not seriously steep – you can see it in the picture on the previous spread, and can check it out more closely while riding the chair to ski the reds from the same point.

Madesimo isn't notably cute, but the setting is prettily wooded; this is the piste to the Lago Azzurro chair-lift

For experts

The top of the Interpista run from Cima Sole is a short but sweet black run.

You'll want to tick off the Canalone run (strictly speaking, requiring proper off-piste precautions – read 'Slopes'). The lift company puts the maximum gradient at 33°; we're sceptical about that, but it maintains black steepness over a drop of about 600m. There are other ways down the same mountainside, some of them more testing, and by traversing left under the cable car you can access another bunch of routes, including some serious ones, which funnel together before crossing the cable car again. There's acres of red-gradient off-piste either side of the Val di Lei chair-lift, over the hill.

The Angeloga run also marked on the piste map is slightly less steep but much longer (10km, they say) and involves some hiking or skinning. You end up in the village of Fraciscio, needing a taxi home.

Heli-skiing is available, they say.

Fancy stuff

There is a fair-sized terrain park near the top of the gondola, Madepark. They say it has something for everyone, and includes a big kicker.

Madesimo – the resort

Madesimo is at the low-key, non-fashionable end of the spectrum of Italian weekend retreats. Most of its visitors (many second-home owners) stay in apartments and private chalets – it has only a dozen hotels, just enough bars and restaurants but no more, hardly any shops. NB There are two roads up from Campodolcino – a spectacularly tortuous one climbing what is virtually a cliff, and a more normal one that's longer but nearly as quick.

Convenience

It's a small village, and with three widely spaced lift stations you're unlikely to be more than 200m from a lift or piste – and there are plenty of places much closer.

Lodgings

The hotels are mostly simple, making for a cheap holiday. We've enjoyed staying at the 2-star K2, close to the gondola station – very good, interesting food. The 3-star Meridiana over the road is naturally a bit smoother, with a spa. We've also enjoyed the 4-star Andossi, a short walk from the Montalto chair-lift and nursery slope – good rooms, pool and breakfast. The 3-star Tambò is on the snow out at Motta.

Bars and restaurants

Acquarela's umbrella bar at mid-mountain does good afternoon business, and gets very lively at weekends. The aperitivo hotspot in the village is the central Bollicine wine/cocktail bar – a great spot. There's a reasonable choice of places to eat. The Osteria Vegia is a lovely old inn doing satisfying traditional dishes; for something more sophisticated, look at the Sport Hotel Alpina's Cantinone – very pleasant despite its Michelin star, with a delicious tasting menu.

Off the slopes

There's a sports centre with climbing walls, squash, volleyball, tennis, fitness facilities and ice skating. The only pool we know of is shared by the Andossi and Alpina hotels.

There are good walks up the dead-end valley and up on to the Andossi plateau north-west of the village. There are some marked snowshoe routes too.

The snowmobiling opportunities here are exceptional, with a vast area to enjoy on the Andossi plateau and on towards Passo Spluga and Switzerland – the routes add up to 70km, they say.

For families

Quite an attractive prospect. The Baby Park Larici at the top of the gondola has a good covered carpet-lift.

Campodolcino 1100m

The Sky Express funicular takes under three minutes to whisk you up 600m to Motta from this unremarkable but not unpleasant little valley town, where you may find lodgings a bit cheaper – though there's not a very wide choice. There are some bars and restaurants, but the place does not resemble a ski resort at all.

Madonna di Campiglio

Madonna di Campiglio / Pinzolo / Marilleva / Folgarida

Campiglio is on the western fringes of the fabulously scenic Dolomites, detached from the core of the region (and from the famous Superski lift pass consortium). It is the senior partner in a ski area linking it with a low valley town (Pinzolo) and two high ski stations (Folgarida and Marilleva).

The area is beautiful, varied and big, not so much in terms of piste km (it gets a middling rating) but in overall dimensions – over 17km from north to south. There are few areas that give a greater sense of travel.

It's an upmarket resort – no rival to Cortina on the shopping front but, with three Michelin-starred restaurants, some way ahead in the gourmet stakes. Happily, it also has plenty of good restaurants for the rest of us.

The mountains in brief

Size Big enough, with a great sense of travel over huge distances

Slopes Gentle open slopes at the top, steep stuff in the woods lower down

Snow Some vulnerable slopes, but excellent snowmaking saves the day

System, Lift Generally efficient, but there are bottlenecks needing attention

Sustenance For a smart, upmarket resort, disappointing; some good spots

For beginners Excellent gentle slopes, although they are out of the village

For true blue skiers Good slopes at Campiglio; other resorts out of bounds

For the confident Lots to do in every sector, including easy blacks

For experts Few challenges on-piste; off-piste is limited (banned, technically)

Fancy stuff The main Ursus park on Passo Grostè is a serious affair

Campiglio – the resort in brief

Convenience Ski-in lodgings can be found, but most people need a bus

Lodgings Something for everyone, including the budget-conscious

Bars and restaurants A wide choice, including several gourmet options

Off the slopes A proper toboggan run (hooray!) but no aquatic centre

For families Could work well if you choose your spot with care

Pass notes	Key facts		Key ratings	
You can save a bit by buying a pass for Campiglio or Pinzolo alone. For a small premium, you can get a Superskirama pass that covers Passo Tonale and several other areas as well as this one. Beginners can pay by the ride or buy points cards.	Altitude	1520m	Size	★★★
	Range	850–2500m	Snow	★★★
	Slopes (see text)	128km	Fast lifts	★★★★
	Where to stay, ideally		Mountain rest's	★★★
	In the heart of the village, between the Pradalago and Cinque Laghi lifts.		Beginner	★★★★
			True blue	★★★
			Confident	★★★★
	Websites		Expert	★★
	campigliodolomiti.it funiviecampiglio.it		Convenience	★★★
			Families	★★★★
			Village charm	★★★★

The mountains in detail

This is a complex, sprawling area, so this overview is bound to be a bit superficial. Campiglio has three main access lifts. From the core of the village at the north end of the resort as a whole, gondolas go roughly north to Pradalago and west to Cinque Laghi; on the east side of the village, across the central park, a third gondola goes to Monte Spinale.

From a point low on the Cinque Laghi slopes, a gondola (with a mid-station towards the south end of the village) links to the Pinzolo slopes on Dos del Sabion (giving great close-up views of the Brenta Dolomites).

North of the village at Grostè, a fast chair goes up to the Pradalago slopes and a gondola in the opposite direction to the high, bare slopes of Passo Grostè, linked in various ways with Monte Spinale.

From Pradalago, runs and lifts go off northwards over Monte Vigo and Monte Spolverino to the modern ski stations of Folgarida and Marilleva, and to Daolasa, which is not a resort but a railway station.

Size

The area claims 150km of pistes. Given the sprawling nature of the area, we'd have been prepared to believe that figure. But Christoph Schahe (read the introduction) puts it a bit lower at 129km. So we added up the figures helpfully provided on the printed piste map, and guess what: they total 128.3km. But in either case, it gets a ✳✳✳ size rating.

Slopes

It's a very diverse area, but mostly it's characterised by open gentle slopes high up and wooded steeper slopes towards the bottom. The Passo Grostè area is the highest and gentlest sector, peaking at a modest 2500m, and rather resembles a glacier, but it's made of rock. The descent from the top to Campiglio is about 6.5km long with a vertical of 980m.

Seen from the gentle, treeless Passo Grostè of the more mixed Pradalago slopes; M Vigo in the shade, right

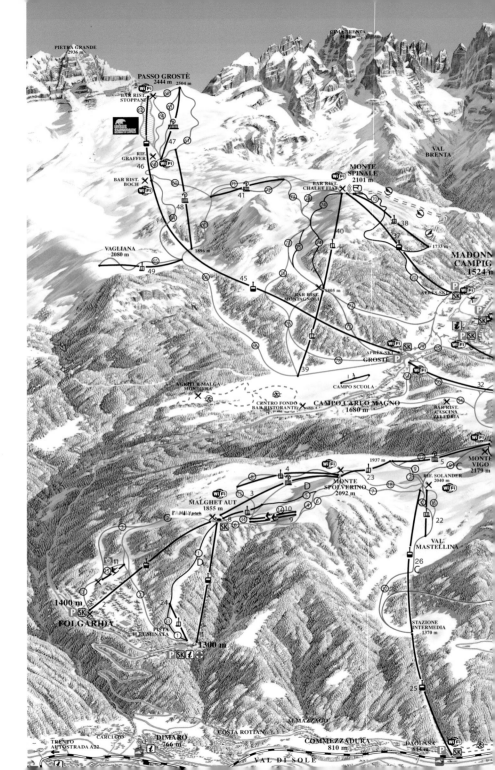

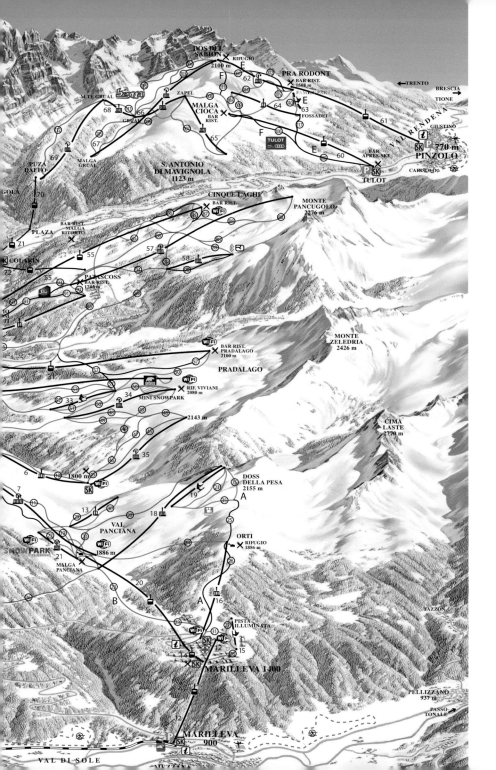

It's not in general an area for very long descents, but the piste map lists some 'cult' descents at the outlying resorts of 4/5/6km, notably Dolomitica Tour from Dos del Sabion to Tulot in the Pinzolo sector– 5.7km, 1250m vertical and largely classified black. The Tulot piste in the same spot is a 2.6km black run served by a single gondola. Laps, anyone?

Snow

By Dolomites standards the snowfall record is not bad. The altitudes are middling, except that Pinzolo is exceptionally low, so the run to Tulot mentioned above is very vulnerable in warm weather. Pinzolo gets afternoon sun, too. Elsewhere, slope orientations vary widely: Marilleva and Folgarida are essentially shady, but the run back towards Campiglio from M Vigo is famously sunny, as is the Amazzonia black piste from Pradalago. Most of the slopes there and at Cinque Laghi get the morning sun, which is not a problem.

Snowmaking is said to cover 95% of the pistes, and we've certainly enjoyed excellent piste skiing here during a drought. The system is able to cover all the slopes in five days, starting from zero.

The north end of the village from Centenario

System, Lift

There are fast lifts in practically all the key positions, and the exceptions are gradually being dealt with. Two ancient double chair-lifts are being replaced by six-seaters as we write in 2019 – on M Spolverino above Folgarida and on M Spinale. This still leaves some irritating slow old chairs in those sectors.

Although it's reasonably fast, the two-stage Grostè gondola is 5.5km long and takes 20 minutes.

At quiet times, the system is queue-free, but at peak times you may find 10-minute queues, or worse in some key spots – especially in the afternoon when the tidal flows between Campiglio and the northern outposts are at their peak. All of the chairs in the M Vigo area are prone to these tidal queues. Some new eight-seaters are needed, really. Meanwhile, it's worth visiting the northerly resorts early in the day, to get home before rush hour.

Sustenance

There are adequate restaurants in all the obvious places, and there are some good ones, but we repeatedly find ourselves a bit disappointed by the lunch options here. Restaurants are marked on the piste map, but many are not named.

A couple of the best places are on the Pradalago slopes – Rif Viviani at the top, and Cascina Zeledria near the bottom (although service was stretched last time we visited). Be aware that the blue run you take to reach the latter has a short gnarly stretch below the restaurant.

We like the look of the calm back room of Chalet Fiat on Spinale – all shiny glasses and crisp linen – and readers approve wholeheartedly. Malga Montagnoli, halfway down the hill, is on our agenda, too.

More on the slopes

For beginners

There are very gentle slopes served by a carpet-lift and a chair-lift on the golf course out at Campo Carlo Magno, a little satellite resort next to the Grostè lift stations. Unless you've chosen lodgings out here, that means riding buses to and fro. Once off the nursery slopes you can progress to lovely gentle runs up the Fortini chair-lift at Pradalago.

For true blue skiers

There's a lot of good skiing to be done, and you can travel quite long distances around Campiglio – but the outlying resorts to the north and south can't be reached on blue runs.

If your confidence is low, the best place to start is on the lovely open slopes at Pradalago; there are two lifts to play on at the top. To get back to the village, take the long blue run 50 to Grostè and the bus from there; run 56 has a tricky bit, and then feeds in to the bottom of 85 from Cinque Laghi, which gets busy and can have choppy snow.

Once you have a bit of confidence you can cheerfully tackle these runs, and the whole of the tougher run 85 from the top of Cinque Laghi. At the top lift station expect to have to force your way through the milling crowd to turn right for the easier start to the run.

On Passo Grostè you can do laps on the top stage of the gondola or on the Grostè fast chair-lift – the reds are just as easy as the blues here – and then tackle the much longer descent on runs 60 and 66 to the village. There are some steeper pitches on the way down, but nothing that strays outside the blue classification. There's also a blue run on the slow Nube d'Argento double chair, and you can ride the chair above it to Monte Spinale and take the interestingly varied blue run 71 to join run 60, perhaps pausing on the way to do some laps on the Boch fast chair.

For confident intermediates

This is a great area for the confident red-run skier. Practically all the red pistes on the map are worthwhile; most are served by fast lifts; and the sense of travel the area offers takes some beating.

The reds at the top of Grostè are indistinguishable from the blues, but the reds lower down in this sector are much more interesting, as is Diretta on Spinale, once it gets off the summit plateau.

The north-facing reds at the top of the Pinzolo slopes are just enjoyable cruises, but those on the flank of the mountain above Pinzolo offer more challenge. When we last visited, we had the two runs on the slow Zapel chair-lift more or less to ourselves – great fun. You might also take a look at the lower part of the black Tulot piste, too, accessed by run 117, Variante Tulot; it was classified red in the past, and really is a borderline case. The run back to the gondola for Campiglio starts as a cruise but steepens at the end.

Cinque Laghi is a classic red hill: the famous FIS 3-Tre race course is an excellent, testing red run, and Centenario and the black Canalone Miramonti below it – regularly used for World Cup slalom races – carry on in the same vein. Nambino from the lower Pancugolo is less challenging but well worthwhile.

The reds on Pradalago are worth a bit of your time, perhaps on your way to the outlying resorts to the north. Take the time, too, to do a lap on the Genziana chair to ski the Genziana piste, much more rewarding than Genziana Bassa which is the natural way to Monte Vigo.

From Monte Vigo you can reach worthwhile reds in several directions; the pick, we reckon, is the run curling down to the Daolasa gondola mid-station. If you're going down to Marilleva, try to find time for a ride on the slow chair to Doss della Pesa, first to ski the worthwhile short red and then maybe to ski the long black Nera Marilleva, which is really a tough red, usually with good snow.

On the way back to Campiglio, Malghette from M Vigo is a fabulously scenic run; it may be fab to ski as well, or it may in parts be rock-hard moguls

(it faces due south). The easy black Amazzonia from Pradalago is south-facing too; it gets a fraction of the traffic, but at the end of the day it may be icy.

For experts

If you read the previous section you'll gather that many of the black pistes are not seriously steep. The top half of the Tulot piste at Pinzolo (aka Dolomitica Star) is said to reach 35° at its steepest. If it does, it's over a short stretch. The final stretch of Spinale Direttissima is credited with the same gradient. The other black on Spinale is nowhere near as steep.

Spinale Direttissima is one of two steep black runs that are left ungroomed for a day after a snowfall. The other is the short Pancugolo on Cinque Laghi, which we suspect is the steepest of the lot.

The off-piste situation is very unsatisfactory. The formal position, confirmed to us by the lift company again in 2019, is that off-piste is forbidden. But bizarrely it seems to be tolerated, and at least some of the ski schools advertise it. It's certainly not a resort for major lift-served off-piste descents, but there are plenty of ski touring routes to undertake.

Fancy stuff

Ursus is a big snow park at the top of Passo Grostè – one of the five best in the Alps, they claim, with features to suit all levels. The Ursus Mini Park at Pradalago is aimed at beginners and near-beginners.

It's a polished, towny village, with the usual evening passeggiata – a more Alpine version of Cortina

Campiglio – the resort

The village is traditional in style, smart without being conspicuously swanky, with a traffic-free central zone that effectively cuts out through-traffic. It spreads down both sides of a neat little park including a small lake, available for skating, to a more spacious suburb at the south end. All of this in a lovely wooded setting, with Dolomite peaks in view.

Convenience

The village is 2.5km long, but the heart of it lies between the Pradalago and Cinque Laghi lift stations, 400m apart at the northern end. Staying in this area also puts you within walking distance of the Spinale gondola station, east of the park. It's possible to find ski-in lodgings, more or less, in the village, and out at Campo Carlo Magno (read the description on the next page). When choosing your location, bear in mind that there is a stream running through the village, and not too many bridges (though it passes under the focal Piazza Righi).

The village is bypassed by a long road tunnel to the west, and the core is traffic-free – arriving by road you need to turn off at the right junction.

Ski-buses run around the village and out to Campo Carlo Magno, frequently at peak times in high season, less frequently at other times. There's a daily charge (€2 in 2019) for these buses; ridiculous.

Lodgings

The majority of hotels are 4-star – there are over 30 of them – but there are plenty of 3-stars, some 2-stars and three 5-stars.

On our last visit we stayed very happily in the very well-run 3-star hotel Alpina, well placed just above the heart of the resort, midway between the main lift stations. The previous time we were equally happy in the 4-star Oberosler, next to the Spinale lift station, with a return piste to the door.

Bars and restaurants

We haven't detected any on-mountain après activity, which is not surprising in this most Italian of resorts. Here, it's all about the passeggiata and the aperitivo. Our regular haunt for a glass of Ferrari is the long-established, highly traditional Suisse bar in the focal Piazza Righi. The hotel Majestic's Lounge Bar nearby is a cooler alternative.

On our last visit we had the rare treat of staying three nights, and found three very satisfactory restaurants. The Roi is a popular, lively restaurant/pizzeria with a woody interior on two floors, at the north end of the village. El Volt in the central hotel Baita is a smaller, calmer, simply decorated place doing good, regionally based food. Antico Focolare, towards the southern end of the village, is a polished place with woody decor, best known for its pizza – and very good they are, too. Other places on our agenda for next time include Convivio, Alfiero and Due Pini.

Three hotels have Michelin-starred restaurants attached – Dolomieu, Gallo Cedrone and Stube Hermitage. No other Italian resort can match that.

Off the slopes

Campiglio is one of the few Italian resorts to have a proper lift-served toboggan run – 2.7km, dropping 340m on Monte Spinale, with trackside restaurants part way down as well as at the top.

There are 22km of cross-country trails up the road at Campo Carlo Magno. There are also long trails in Val di Sole, either side of Marilleva 900. Given the right temperatures, there is skating on the lake in the central park. There are lots of walking paths, along the valleys and up into the slopes – there's a printed guide.

The school gym offers tennis and a climbing wall, among other things. Some hotels have spas and pools open to the public. (Or, the resort suggests rather desperately, you can travel 20km down the valley to the pools in Spiazzo.)

For families

Pick your spot and it should work well. The central park has its attractions, particularly if the weather permits skating on the lake. But you might judge that being close to the snow at Campo Carlo Magno is a better basis for a family holiday. You might also want to look for a hotel with a pool.

Alternatives to Campiglio

Campo Carlo Magno is a mini-resort by the nursery slopes on the low pass north of the village – an obviously attractive location for beginners.

Pinzolo, a low valley town to the south, and Marilleva and Folgarida to the north share an obvious drawback: they are poor starting points for full exploration of the ski area. It's possible to ski to the other end and spend some time there but, given the choice, a base in Campiglio has obvious advantages. It will usually cost more, of course. All three are also a poor choice for blue-run skiers – or for ambitious beginners.

Campo Carlo Magno 1680m

This outpost, 3km away from Campiglio and 130m higher, offers proximity to the nursery slopes and lifts to the Passo Grostè and Pradalago sectors. There are hotels at the Grostè lift base itself, and dotted along the road, up to 1km away. The 4-star hotel Golf is on the nursery slopes and close to the lifts – it's almost ski-in, and only a short plod out. You can walk into the village, but it's quite a hike back up.

Pinzolo 780m

Campiglio is in the comune of Pinzolo, the main town of Val Rendena, 15km away to the south; it's at half the altitude of Campiglio – exceptionally low for a ski resort in this part of the world. The valley road goes through the centre, but it is not an unpleasant place. It has no particular attractions, apart from a hockey-size ice rink. In Carisolo up the valley there's a sports centre with tennis, gym, climbing wall etc. There's a wellness centre with a pool down the valley at Caderzone.

There are plenty of places to stay, and plenty of those are dotted around the northern part of the town within walking distance of the gondola to Prà Rodont at mid-mountain. Here there are excellent beginner facilities, but there is not much easy skiing to progress to, and blue-run skiers can't access Campiglio.

There's a snow park on the back of the hill. There is no piste to the valley here, although there is a black piste further up the valley at Tulot.

Most of the hotels (over 25) are 3-stars, but there are plenty of 4-stars too.

Marilleva 900m/1400m

The major part of Marilleva is a modern ski station at 1400m, at the bottom of a long red run from Monte Vigo. As you ski down to it you see several functional low-rise buildings, but there are many more of these spreading down the hillside in the woods. 1400 is reached from the smaller component of the resort, at 900m on the valley floor, by road or by gondola. There is no piste down. 900 is a small collection of hotels and apartment residences around a railway station – the end of a line, more or less, from Trento that also has a station at the Daolasa gondola.

There's a nursery slope at 1400 served by a drag-lift, and another higher on the mountain at Val Panciana; but there's nowhere to go from there without skiing red runs. At the same spot there's a 250m-long snow park, and a special family park.

Folgarida 1300m/1400m

Folgarida is more traditional in style than Marilleva. It is another two-part resort, but these two parts are close together. 1400 is a lift station (and not much else) beside the road from Campiglio to Val di Sole. 1300 is a mini-resort set off the road, with some quite smart hotels and shops. Both have gondolas up to the large, busy mid-mountain lift station of Malghet Aut.

There are excellent beginner slopes up at Malghet Aut, and a special family park. But where do you go from there? Read on.

Blue run skiers tempted to stay here by the runs shown on the map from M Spolverino and Malghet Aut should proceed with caution. It's obvious from the map that you can't get much further than the peak on blue runs. What's not obvious is that the blue from M Spolverino to Malghet Aut is rather tricky on the upper part, and so is the otherwise lovely run from Malghet Aut to Folgarida 1300. We'd go so far as to say that this part of the run probably should be red.

Monterosa – Champoluc

Champoluc / Stafal / Gressoney la Trinité / Alagna

Monterosa is an extraordinary ski area close to Monte Rosa itself. It combines a lot of high off-piste terrain with a long, narrow, three-valley piste network linking widely separated villages.

Champoluc at the western end is the main resort of the area, with the biggest area of local slopes and the widest range of lodgings – but it is still a pleasantly low-key, low-glitz village. You can easily ski the whole area from here, so we attach little importance to the central location of Gressoney and Stafal. Bad weather can close the high lifts, and Alagna in the eastern valley then has very little skiing to offer. Why risk it?

A plan to build a gondola to Cervinia/Zermatt is gathering momentum.

The mountains in brief

Size Quite limited piste km, but spread over a huge area – 16km across
Slopes Wide variety; mainly open, but with two wooded areas
Snow Feast or famine off-piste, but good snowmaking and great grooming
System, Lift Mainly fast, with some exceptions; queue-free on weekdays
Sustenance Lots of decent places, and some rather special ones.
For beginners Great slopes, but progression is not straightforward
For true blue skiers All a bit tricky if you are lacking in confidence
For the confident Splendid long runs for cruising and carving
For experts Given good snow (and touring kit, ideally), it's fabulous
Fancy stuff A funslope halfway to Gressoney, and a snow park further on

Champoluc – the resort in brief

Convenience Depends where you stay, and with whom; buses are not great
Lodgings A good range of options, now including an unusual five-star
Bars and restaurants Some pleasant bars and excellent restaurants
Off the slopes Not the most entertaining of resorts
For families Quiet ambience and good nursery slopes are a good start

Pass notes	Key facts		Key ratings	
A six-day pass covers two days in other resorts in the Aosta valley. A full valley pass is available. For the top Indren cable car you pay a supplement, weekly or daily. Beginners can buy half-day and day passes for the carpet-lifts at Crest and Frachey plus the access lifts.	Altitude	1580m	Size	**
	Range	1200–3275m	Snow	****
	Slopes (see text)	80km	Fast lifts	****
			Mountain rest's	****
	Where to stay, ideally		Beginner	**
	A stroll from the Champoluc gondola station.		True blue	**
			Confident	****
	Websites		Expert	****
	visitmonterosa.com		Convenience	**
			Families	****
			Village charm	***

The mountains in detail

Champoluc's local slopes are in two linked sectors, one directly above the village (mostly above the mid-mountain area of Crest), the other up the valley above Ciarcerio, reached by a short funicular from a car park at Frachey. From there, the main network goes east over Colle Bettaforca to Stafal, then via Gabiet over Passo Salati to Alagna. Each of the four mountainsides has basically a single piste, red or red/black.

Above Alagna there's a short blue run at the top and a short red one at Pianalunga, at mid-mountain. In the central valley there is a more extensive area of low wooded slopes above Gressoney.

The lift pass covers several other small areas including Antagnod, 4 km down the valley from Champoluc. The Indren cable car from Passo Salati, the key to much of the best off-piste terrain, now requires extra payment.

Size

The current Monterosa website is so flaky that we've given up trying to establish what piste extent the area currently claims. On the Valle d'Aosta site, the familiar, fantastic figure of 180km for the whole lift pass area is still being promoted, although we established long ago that this figure overstates the extent by 100%. After we spelled this out in *Where to Ski and Snowboard 2011*, the lift company halved its published length figures for individual runs, producing a total for the linked area (at that time) of 73km. Since then, Christoph Schrahe (read the book's intro) has published a figure of 80km. Either of these lower figures gives us a ✳✳ size rating.

Slopes

As the map suggests, these are red-gradient mountains, with blue runs only in certain locations. (The green 'pistes' on the map are ski touring routes, for climbing.) Most of the skiing is on open slopes; but the lower slopes at Champoluc/Frachey and at Gressoney, have extensive wooded areas.

There are some good long runs, notably from Passo Salati to Alagna – about 7km for a vertical of 1760m (when snow permits: it's low and sunny at the end). The descent to Stafal offers 1140m.

Snow

The snowfall record looks reasonable on average, and pretty good at altitude, but (as in many Italian areas) it can be rather erratic. For the off-piste it's best to book at short notice. There are some runs (eg at Crest and from Passo Salati to Gressoney) that get an undesirable amount of sun, but a lot of the skiing is high (a lot of the off-piste, in particular), and there is snowmaking where it's needed (eg the Champoluc home run).

System, Lift

All the key lifts in the three-valley network are fast, but there are slow lifts in a few spots. Most irritating are the long chairs in the woods at Gressoney. Less important are the Bocchetta chair at Pianalunga, the top chair at Champoluc and the link between Champoluc and Frachey – these last two can be avoided by starting and ending your day at Frachey.

On weekdays, the slopes are crowd-free and queues are not a problem. But there are some bottlenecks that cause problems on fine weekends. The Alpe Mandria quad chair-lift at Ciarcerio needs an upgrade: it serves popular runs and is also needed by skiers on their way to Gressoney and skiers on their way to Champoluc via the slow linking chair-lift mentioned above. That chair shifts a miserable 900 people an hour, so you may meet a second queue there.

The lifts to Passo Salati can have queues. The cable car from Pianalunga is quite big, but it is also long and shifts only 800 people an hour. The upper stage was duplicated in 2017 by a fast quad

chair, solving the queue problem at the Cimalegna mid-station (now redundant). The gondola from Gabiet can't always meet demand.

In 2018 the gondola out of Champoluc was upgraded and extended to reach the upper gondola, cutting out a tedious walk.

You can ski off-piste down a long deserted valley to the Champoluc valley from the top of the Valtournenche slopes, linked to Cervinia and to Zermatt in Switzerland, and the long-standing plan for a gondola link from Frachey up that valley seems to be gaining support. It would be about 8km long; quite a project, and quite a boost for Champoluc.

Sustenance

There are countless places for lunch, most of them good, some quite special. Restaurants are named on the piste map.

At Champoluc there are three lovely places in old stone huts – Stadel Soussun above Frachey, Aroula above Crest and Frantze Le Rascard below Crest – the last being our favourite in the whole area. At Frachey, we've also enjoyed the modern Campo Base. Above Gressoney, Punta Jolanda is a regular haunt – a lively spot with good food and great views. Above Alagna we've somehow failed to spend any time in the higher restaurants, but often seem to end up having a very satisfactory lunch at Shoppf Wittine, in a fine spot beside the home piste.

Reader tips include Edelweiss at Crest 2727, Soleil at the top of the Frachey funicular, Mandria higher up at Frachey, Colle Bettaforca, Sitten above S Anna, Morgenrot low down in the woods at Gressoney, Rifugio Gabiet and Schene Biel at Gabiet, Stolemberg at Passo Salati and the Baita at Pianalunga.

More on the slopes

For beginners

At Crest there is a splendid beginner area, with two long carpet-lifts serving gentle slopes, and several restaurants nearby for R&R. Unfortunately, there is no long blue run to progress to. At Ciarcerio there is a shorter carpet-lift, and the Mandria chair-lift accesses the Lago blue run; this is easier than the reds at Crest, but it's not ideal – although mostly gentle, it has a steeper section. It's worth thinking about making the quarter-hour trip to Antagnod. Here there are short and long carpet-lifts, and gentler blue runs served by a short slow chair-lift and a fast longer one.

The wooded slopes at Gressoney are good in bad weather (with a fine lunch spot at Punta Jolanda)

For true blue skiers

It's not an ideal area if you're lacking confidence. A glance at the map shows that you can't get around the area on blue runs. The only genuine blue run locally is Lago at Ciarcerio, discussed above. Many of the reds are at the easy end of the scale and might be blue in France, and some relative novices are happy to tackle them. Grooming is excellent, which helps.

The reds from Colle Bettaforca are of red gradient only at the start, and someone who is confident on most blues could tackle them, given the necessary encouragement. To get to them you do have to deal with a steeper pitch on the Liaison red piste from the top of the Mandria chair.

The blue runs from Passo Salati to Cimalegna are lovely, and now served by a fast chair. But whether they justify the hassle of getting there and back is another question – the return red run is pretty steep (and sunny, affecting the snow), so you'll be riding gondolas all the way down to Stafal.

For confident intermediates

This is a great area for cruising and carving on long, quiet, easy, well-groomed red runs, provided you don't mind cruising and carving on the same runs repeatedly. For a bit more of a challenge, head for the runs on the Mandria chair, the infamous 'goat' run link from Sarezza towards Frachey (it has a steep and narrow start) and the runs either side of Passo Salati – the Olen run from there towards Alagna was optimistically classified red when it was first converted from off-piste status in the early years of the century; it was soon altered to black but barely merits the classification. The Moos black run to Stafal is basically a red run with just one short steep pitch.

The home run to Champoluc is a decent red, and those in the wooded area above Gressoney are also rewarding.

For experts

As we've suggested above, the black runs are not serious, but they're steep enough to be good fun when the snow is good. The short one at the top of the Jolanda chair at Gressoney is the steepest.

More importantly, Monterosa is famed for its off-piste skiing, touring and heli-skiing. There is plenty to do with straight Alpine kit, but touring kit opens up many more options. We can do no more than skim the surface here.

Without going further than the top of the Champoluc lifts you can access worthwhile routes in several directions. Above Frachey, from Colle Bettaforca there is plenty of space either side of the lift, and more serious adventures on the Gressoney side. Gressoney's local lifts access many routes in and out of the trees. From Gabiet, at mid-mountain on the way to Passo Salati, there are multiple ways down on skier's left of the gondola from Stafal, and a lovely run from the Lago chair-lift to Gressoney-la-Trinité.

And then you come to Passo Salati and the Indren cable car to the high point of the area at 3275m. There are multiple options from the top. The dotted line on the piste map is no longer explained on the map; it is a popular route that is often skied into a piste-like state, but it is emphatically not a piste. There are many more serious routes in the same direction and in the opposite direction towards Alagna, involving a bit of climbing – including the classic La Balma.

Old hands will remember that the top part of this was once a long black piste from Punta Indren, served by an ancient cable car with the assistance of a rickety bucket-lift to get you back to the base station. Now, you have no option but to go on down to Alagna.

Without riding the Indren cable car there is plenty to do from the Passo, including very challenging stuff, with and without climbing. Then, way down the Olen valley the Bocchetta chair-lift to the old cable car station provides another way into the lower Balma bowl.

The woods at Frachey and Gressoney offer plenty of options for bad weather days, to get you in shape for the higher stuff when the weather clears.

Heli-lifts open up countless routes on the Monte Rosa massif, including descents to Zermatt, returning via the Zermatt lifts and an off-piste run down the deserted valley from the top of the Valtournenche lifts.

Fancy stuff

On the Stafal side of Colle Bettaforca there is now a funslope. Recently the only snow park for grown-ups has been beyond Stafal, at Gabiet.

Champoluc – the resort

Champoluc is one of the most unspoiled, low-key resorts you will come across. At the lift base there is micro-resort – a 200m stretch of small shops and restaurants – and there are hotels and bars dotted along the approach to that from the centre. But the rest of the village seems barely affected by resorthood – a spacious sprawl of chalet-style buildings ancient and modern, with a church and a petrol station at its heart.

Although it has now been discovered by other operators – Inghams and sister companies have chalet hotels here – Champoluc was brought to the UK market by the smaller operator Ski 2 in 1999; they're still here, doing a great job, with their own British-staffed ski school and on-call minibuses.

Convenience

The lift station is 700m from the church, and many lodgings are on or near the one-way paved road between the two; but there are places further away – the most recently built hotels are up to 1km away, outside the village, halfway to the alternative lift station at Frachey.

There are ski-buses between the lift stations (and serving Antagnod) roughly every half hour, but life is complicated by the one-way traffic system – the buses from Frachey to Antagnod don't pass the Champoluc lift station. The better hotels run shuttles, as does tour operator Ski 2.

Lodgings

There are over 20 hotels, ranging from very simple places to the latest addition, the 5-star CampZero – a cutting-edge place that, sorry to say, left us unimpressed in various respects. We prefer the woody 4-star La Rouja – or the creaky old 3-star Villa Anna Maria.

For some years the hotel Champoluc, in pole position at the bottom of the piste, has been run by Inghams as a catered chalet hotel. For 2019/20 it is also being offered by family holiday specialist Esprit. Ski Total also has a chalet hotel – the lovely hotel Breithorn.

Champoluc is an unspoiled valley village; its nursery slopes are at Crest, above the trees, reached by gondola

Out of the ordinary

The three special mountain restaurants we mentioned earlier – Frantze Le Rascard, Aroula and Stadel Soussun – all have bedrooms. Hotellerie de Mascognaz is a restored/converted old hamlet, isolated above the village at 1800m and reached by 4WD or snowmobile.

Bars and restaurants

It's a quiet place, but there are some animated bars. We roped in Ski 2's Simon Brown for guidance. Simon tips Rifugio Belvedere or Bruno's, low down on the home piste, for a final pint on the piste; then at the base, Kondor (previously Atelier Gourmand) or the Bistro, both with free nibbles. Later on, Simon suggests the Golosone or the bar of hotel California for live music. His favourite places for dinner are the cosy Essentiel da Andreone in central Champoluc, and the Grange or the Petit Coq up the valley at Frachey, both doing a range of local dishes. Churen is the main pizzeria.

Off the slopes

There's a smart modern spa just outside the village with an indoor/outdoor pool. The hotel CampZero has a climbing wall. There's cross-country skiing down the valley at Brusson, and walks (with or without snowshoes) in various spots. There's no sign of organised toboggan runs, and the skating rink is no more.

For families

It's fine for families. If we were taking kids, we'd plug in to the facilities offered by tour operator Ski 2, which has its own ski school. And we'd pick a hotel close to the spa/pool (or with its own).

Alternatives to Champoluc

Gressoney is near the head of the central valley of the area. (Gressoney-la-Trinité, to be precise – Gressoney-St-Jean is just down the valley.) Practically at the head is the outpost of Stafal – the main lift base, and the obvious place to stay if your priority is access to the three-valley system.

Alagna may suit experts fixing an off-piste break at short notice, but the very limited local piste skiing is a problem for others.

Stafal 1830m

The dominant feature of Stafal is its car parks, filling the narrow valley bottom. There's nothing resembling a village – just a few hotels dotted around the margins. We've enjoyed staying at the modern hotel Nordend, a B&B place a short walk from the lifts, with attached restaurant and après bar.

There's a short carpet-lift at the lift base; after that, it's up to Passo Salati.

Gressoney-la-Trinité 1640m

For skiing purposes, Gressoney is a collection of apartments and hotels clustered around the Punta Jolanda chair-lift station. This is a great place to be based on a snowy day, less good when you're itching to go cruising the main network or hitting the Indren cable car – the Stafal lifts are two long slow chairs and a black run away. This cluster is slightly separate from the original village, which is neat and unspoiled but seems a bit lifeless in winter – though it has a big natural ice rink. The hotels Dufour and Jolanda Sport, right next to the lift, have been recommended by readers.

There are two carpet-lifts near the lift station. After that, it's Passo Salati.

Alagna 1200m

Alagna is a small, quiet, unspoiled village with some lovely old wooden farmhouses in the Walser style – echoed in the design of the cool, modern Alagna Experience Resort 4-star hotel. The polished hotel Cristallo and the historic hotel Monterosa are close together in the surprisingly towny centre, near the pretty church.

The Shoppf Wittine is a good place to stop for a beer on the home piste. Dir und Don is the pivotal bar-restaurant.

There are beginner lifts up at Pianalunga (at mid-mountain) and on a separate area at Wold, a mile up the valley. After that, it's up to Passo Salati.

Note that Alagna is reached from the east, not from the Valle d'Aosta like the other Monterosa resorts.

Pila

The great curving trench of the Aosta valley contains one of the main concentrations of ski resorts in Italy – and one of them is above the sizeable town of Aosta itself. A gondola from just outside the centre rises 1200m (via two intermediate stations) to a purpose-built development high on the mountains to the south: Pila. It's the nearest thing in Italy to a French purpose-built resort – convenient for skiing (up to a point), but lacking charm. Aosta is something else – like so many Italian towns, it has a cute historic core and at least one huge piazza. The gondola works from 8am to 5pm; the ride takes only 18 minutes.

    The skiing is nicely varied, high and shady. It's limited in extent, but the pass covers two days out in other Valle d'Aosta resorts, eg La Thuile.

The mountains in brief

Size It's small – the smallest resort in these pages to get a ✶✶ rating

Slopes A good mix of terrain, largely wooded but open at the top

Snow More snowmaking is needed to keep upper runs open

System, Lift You can do a lot on fast lifts, but there are too many slow ones

Sustenance Not a bad selection, for such a small area

For beginners Good slopes in two locations; progression runs OK

For true blue skiers Very limited unless you are happy to tackle easy reds

For the confident A good mixture of cruisers and more challenging pistes

For experts Some genuine black runs, and good off-piste beside them

Fancy stuff The park is big and varied

Pila – the resort in brief

Convenience Not entirely convenient – worth picking your spot

Lodgings Several run-of-the-mill hotels, but nothing swanky

Bars and restaurants An adequate range for a short stay

Off the slopes Not a lot to do, but there's tubing and sledging in the fun park

For families The fun park and the central nursery slope are a good start

Pass notes	Key facts		Key ratings	
A six-day pass covers two days in any other resort in the Aosta valley. A full valley pass is available. Beginners can buy a cheaper pass covering the village carpet lifts and the chair-lift that runs up the side of the village.	Altitude	1800m	Size	✶✶
	Range	1800–2740m	Snow	✶✶✶
	Slopes (see text)	50km+	Fast lifts	✶✶
	Where to stay, ideally		Mountain rest's	✶✶✶
	Near the bottom or the top of the Pila-Gorraz liaison chair-lift.		Beginner	✶✶✶
			True blue	✶✶
			Confident	✶✶✶
	Websites		Expert	✶✶
	pila.it		Convenience	✶✶✶
			Families	✶✶✶
			Village charm	✶

The mountains in detail

The village, at the top of the gondola from Aosta, sits at the bottom of a high, shady bowl beneath a steep ridge peaking at the 3090m Pointe Valletta (well away from the skiing). At the bottom of the village, the Chamolé chair serves wooded runs from about 2300m but is also the quick way to Gorraz, at the top of the village (there is a slow chair alternative, much used by novices). From Gorraz, the fast Leissé chair serves much of the central part of the area, and accesses the slow Couis 1 chair to the top (about 2700m); to looker's right, a cable car climbs gently to three more chair-lifts, the highest of them reaching 2600m, not far short of the ridge.

When snow is good, a red run drops 260m from the village to the upper of two mid-stations of the access gondola, at Plan Praz.

Size

The resort claims 70km of pistes, a figure we found a bit unlikely. But the resort helpfully provides individual piste lengths on its mountain map. These add up to 50km, which feels nearer the mark. But they exclude the half-dozen linking tracks labelled R on the map, which in most resorts would be included in the reckoning. These would take the total over 50km, and push the resort into the bottom end of our ✷✷ size category.

Slopes

A very distinctive feature of the mountain is the height of the treeline. The Chamolé chair to 2310m just about reaches it. Basically, it's only the runs from the two highest lifts that are out of the trees.

Much of the mountain is of red gradient, with blue runs cutting across the slope, but the centre of the bowl is relatively gentle. Above the trees, it's steeper, as the map suggests.

It's not an area for notably long runs, but there are multiple ways to get a descent of several km in length and 800m vertical – and the Grimod blue run from the upper mountain to the bottom of the village racks up almost 6km.

The heavy dotted lines on the map are not runs, but ski mountaineering routes, for climbing on skins.

Snow

The experts say Pila gets its snow from Mediterranean storms, which generally translates into a more erratic snow record

than those of resorts further north, which are more affected by Atlantic weather. Certainly, in terms of average snowfall Pila is not a match for Courmayeur or La Thuile. But the altitudes and orientation (nearly all slopes facing north-east to north-west) are good, and most of the pistes are covered by snowmaking (given a yellow highlight on the map). Among the exceptions are most of the high black pistes, and the runs on the Grimondet chair on the extreme right of the map. When we visited in mid-January several worthwhile runs were closed.

System, Lift

This is a distinct weakness of the area: there is a lot of room for improvement here. The 2km Leissé chair-lift up the middle of the area and the two chair-lifts on looker's left of the map are fast. So is the Grand Grimod cable car on the right, of course (although its capacity is low). So you can do a lot of skiing in the middle and left of the map on fast lifts. But the other five chairs, at the top of the hill and on looker's right of the map, are all slow – and some are long. The two top chairs, Couis 1 and Couis 2, are about a mile long and the rides take about 15 long, cold minutes.

Sustenance

There are lots of places to eat in the village, of course, but also half a dozen up on the slopes – plenty for an area of this size. They're not named on the map.

The most interesting and possibly the best is Société (Société Anonyme de Consommation, in full) on skier's left of the Nouva chair – three different rooms, from a modern bar to a little beamed 'snug', with a varied, adventurous menu. Across the hill at the bottom of the Couis 2 chair, the Baoutson offers strong competition in a more traditional vein. The self-service Hermitage is tipped, too.

More on the slopes

For beginners

There are carpet-lifts on gentle slopes in two locations: out of the way just below the gondola station and up at Gorraz, at the top of the village. Readers complain of through traffic here, but there is also a quiet piste. These and the Pila-Gorraz liaison chair-lift, linking the two and serving a very gentle blue run 700m long, are covered by a special beginners' day pass. There are some long blue runs higher up to progress to.

Most of the slopes are below the unusually high treeline, and give grand views across the Valle d'Aosta

For true blue skiers

The map shows just two blue runs. The 2km Châtelaine (5) left of the middle of the map is correctly classified but quite challenging. The longer Grimod (15) starting a bit higher on the right is a bit daunting just at the very top, but after that it is a gentle blue – wide where it runs beside the Grimod chair, then a narrow track through the woods before opening out again above the resort. You can avoid the challenging start by starting from the cable car rather than the Leissé chair.

So there's not a lot to do if Châtelaine is about your limit. But if you are happy skiing Châtelaine, you might move on to some of the easiest reds, perhaps starting with Leissé from the eponymous chair or Plan de l'Eyvie from the Nouva chair.

For confident intermediates

Putting aside the limited size of the area – remember, it only just scrapes in to the ✳✳ category – there are lots of worthwhile runs for the confident skier.

The pistes on and around the fast, long Leissé chair and the shorter Nouva six-pack are easy cruises. Pré Noir is a good, long run where you can rack up the miles if the lifts are queue-free. For more of a test, laps on the Du Bois and Gorraz pistes on the fast, long Chamolé chair are called for. The Chamolé piste has steep stretches too, but gets the afternoon sun at the end and has no snowmaking; last time we visited – in January 2019 – it was closed. The runs on the right of the map are worth some rides on the slow Grimondet and Couis 2 chairs, too – but the Grimondet pistes also lack snowmaking, and were closed last time we visited. The top part of Couis 1 from the eponymous slow chair is a waste of time – a winding cat track.

For experts

Basically there are four black runs from the high lifts, all of them genuine blacks. One, Platta de Grevon, was newly created only a few years ago, and is reached from the top of the Couis 1 chair-lift via a covered carpet-lift up the ridge. This is a fine shady, varied run with one seriously steep pitch part way down, which is left ungroomed for some days after a snowfall. Tsa Creuisa, branching from the nearby red run, offers a more sustained challenge although it probably doesn't reach quite the same maximum gradient. From the Couis 2 chair, Bellevue has a steep pitch after an initial traverse, but then mellows. To skier's left, Resselin (aka Direttissima) is the steepest of the four – very tricky when the snow is hard.

The lie of the land doesn't lend itself to major off-piste routes, but there are good open slopes accessible from the two top chairs, some of them seriously steep. Roughly speaking there are three main ways down from each chair.

Fancy stuff

The Areaeffe snow park, on the Grimod chair at the top of the cable car, is big (600m long) and varied, with features for every level.

Pila – the resort

Pila is a curious mixture of individual hotels and guest houses, built in traditional style and dotted around the sloping site, and big, functional apartment residences partly built in to the slope. It doesn't have any central focus or village atmosphere; it's just a place to sleep, really.

The gondola doesn't work in the evenings, and it's only on high-season Wednesdays and weekends that there is a free minibus service instead.

Convenience

Some of the lodgings are ski-in, or nearly so, but not all, by any means. Although it's a small resort it is quite spread out – it's about 1 km long and over 150m vertical from bottom to top. If you're looking at lodgings towards the bottom, be sure you know how you're going to get to a lift.

Lodgings

There are half-a-dozen 3-star hotels; none of them stands out. Chalet des Alpes is handy for the nursery slope below the gondola station, and the Lion Noir has a good position above the Chamolé lift base; it also has a small swimming pool, which may be a clincher for a family.

Bars and restaurants

It's a quiet place in the evening. The mountain restaurants close to village level are popular at close of play, and there's an Oirish pub, Gallagher's, in the centre. There are a couple of restaurants with interesting menus doing very satisfactory dinners – the Yeti and Piazzetta, both close to the gondola station. The Locanderia and. Brasserie du Grimod do excellent pizza.

Off the slopes

We got very excited when we saw a dotted line on the piste map disappearing down the mountain, bearing a toboggan symbol. Sadly, it turns out to be a cartographic cock-up – it's the shuttle-bus route to Aosta. But there is sledging to be had in the Chacard fun park, an excellent area in the middle of the village, with a carpet-lift (and a separate slope for tubing).

Residents of the hotel Lion Noir have a swimming pool available, and the ski pass covers entry to the public pool down in Aosta. Ice skating also requires descent to Aosta.

Snowshoe routes run across the mountainside through woods and up into the ski slopes.

For families

With easy access to snow and the good fun park (see above) in the heart of the village, it's a good choice.

The Aosta option

If you like the idea of staying in a real, interesting town and don't mind starting and ending your day with an 18-minute gondola ride, staying in Aosta is an attractive option. It also makes a better starting point for trips to other resorts.

Aosta dates from ancient Roman times and has lots of monuments from that and later eras. It is the main town of the valley, and the shopping opportunities are impressive. Among its facilities are a hockey-size ice rink and a 25m swimming pool. There are dozens of restaurants including the Michelin-starred Vecchio Ristoro. The simpler Osteria da Nando suits us nicely.

There are plenty of hotels, including a handful of 4-stars and rather more 3-star and 2-star places. The gondola station is over the railway on the south side of the centre, and the 4-star Duca d'Aosta, for example, is 300m from the railway station. There are lockers for skis and boots at both bottom and top gondola stations.

You could be in France. For something more distinctively Italian, stay down in Aosta and ride up each day

Ponte di Legno-Tonale

Passo Tonale / Ponte di Legno

Passo Tonale, the main resort of this recently rebranded area, is a budget resort with good slopes for learning or building confidence, at high altitude – so good snow conditions can be expected (although not guaranteed: it gets a lot of sun, and on our recent March visit we found sheet ice).

What's more, the area has an unusual range of skiing options – a little glacier area to add a bit of high-mountain adventure, and the lower, steeper, wooded slopes of Ponte di Legno for bad-weather days.

Ponte di Legno is a pleasant, handsome village with lodgings dotted around its suburbs – for confident skiers aiming to spend time in the woods, an attractive alternative to bleak, rather charmless Passo Tonale.

The mountains in brief

Size The area only just scrapes into our ✱✱ category; outings are possible

Slopes Very varied, from open easy slopes to challenges in the trees

Snow The main slopes are very sunny but altitudes and snowmaking help

System, Lift Pretty good at Tonale, less so at Ponte di Legno

Sustenance Mountain restaurants are not a highlight

For beginners It would be perfect if there weren't so many beginners here

For true blue skiers Very limited unless you feel able to tackle easy reds

For the confident Lots to do, within the limits of a rather small area

For experts Some epic descents and serious challenges

Fancy stuff A long snow park conveniently placed on the home slopes

Passo Tonale – the resort in brief

Convenience Purpose-built for skiers, but not purpose-designed

Lodgings Dominated by 3-star hotels and apartments

Bars and restaurants A good choice of lively bars, not so many restaurants

Off the slopes Not a strong point – non-skiers should look elsewhere

For families Fine if you find lodgings close to the snow

Pass notes	Key facts		Key ratings	
Alternatives to the local Adamello pass: the Valadaski six-day pass also covers two days in Aprica, an hour to the west; the Combi 1 pass covers a day in Pejo or Madonna di Campiglio, or several other areas; the Superskirama pass covers any number of such days. Beginners can buy points cards valid on all lifts.	Altitude (Tonale)	1880m	Size	✱✱
	Range	1121–2992m	Snow	✱✱✱✱
	Slopes (see text)	62km	Fast lifts	✱✱✱✱
			Mountain rest's	✱✱✱
	Where to stay, ideally		Beginner	✱✱✱✱
	On the snow at the eastern end of the village.		True blue	✱✱✱
			Confident	✱✱✱✱
	Websites		Expert	✱✱✱
	pontedilegnotonale.com		Convenience	✱✱✱
			Families	✱✱✱
			Village charm	✱✱

The mountains in detail

Passo Tonale (still the senior partner in the area, despite the rebranding) has a very simple area of home slopes: an array of chair-lifts of various lengths on a sunny mountainside, two of them leading to higher chairs up to about 2500m. Across the pass road, a chain of gondolas goes up to the Presena glacier, peaking at a few metres short of 3000m.

Ponte di Legno has three lift bases. From Passo Tonale a piste goes to one, isolated in woods, and a gondola makes a link with the main lift station. The third base is 3km and 100m vertical down the valley at Temù. Chair-lifts link the sectors at altitude, peaking at about 1900m.

Size

The resort claims 100km of pistes – a nice round, memorable number that we doubted. The lengths helpfully published on the resort's website total a more reasonable 62km, giving a size rating of ✶✶. (They give lengths for the off-piste runs and ski-touring routes on the piste map too, and these add up to 39km – perhaps that's how they got 100km.)

Slopes

The three sectors are quite different. Passo Tonale's home slopes are gentle at the bottom, steeper at the top. The Presena sector has intermediate slopes at the top and a black run to the valley. Both of these sectors are treeless. Ponte di Legno's area peaks at much the same altitude as the village of Passo Tonale, and the slopes are largely in trees.

The lifts and runs that most people at Tonale spend most of their time on are short, with very limited vertical. The 4.5km red Alpino piste dropping 750m on skier's right of the sector is a splendid exception. And from the glacier you can ski all the way down to the Ponte di Legno link, a descent of 1700m vertical and something like 10km. At Ponte di Legno there are descents to the valley stations in the order of 800m or 900m vertical, and about 3km in length.

On the shady side of the resort is the taller, narrower, steeper sector; the Presena glacier is just out of sight

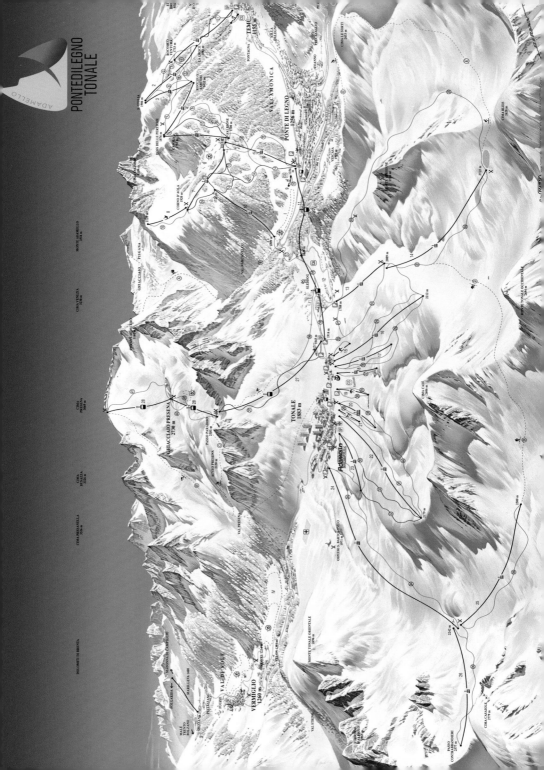

The piste map has dotted lines showing three lift-served off-piste routes and two ski-mountaineering routes. Note that all of the marked runs are pure off-piste routes, with no protection.

Snow

Not surprisingly, given the altitude and the pass location, the snowfall record of Passo Tonale is good by local standards, and there is a lot of snowmaking. The orientation of the main slopes is naturally of some concern later in the season. Lower Ponte di Legno doesn't get nearly so much snow, especially at resort level, but at least its slopes are shady.

System, Lift

Fast quad chairs with covers are the dominant form of lift. Three of the chairs on the main slopes at Tonale are slow, but only one of these is an irritant – Nigritella, on skier's right. At Ponte di Legno things aren't so good: both the chairs making the links between the runs above Ponte di Legno and those above Temù are slow, and all three of the lifts on looker's left of the Ponte di Legno sector are slow. Recognising that most visitors will spend most of their time at Tonale, we're generously awarding ✱✱✱✱.

Neither we nor readers have had problems with queues. But the central lifts on the home slopes can get busy. And the gondola from Ponte di Legno can be very busy on high-season afternoons.

Sustenance

There are few mountain restaurants on the main Tonale slopes – most people eat at the lift bases or in the village. In the other sectors they are dotted around at lift junctions. Few stand out.

The Faita, a little way down the piste towards Ponte di Legno, gets good reports from readers, as does Malga Valbiolo, high on skier's left of the home slopes. At the top of the glacier, Panorama 3000 is a cool glass and steel affair with great views. At Ponte di Legno, the table-service part of the rustic Valbione is very good when not rammed, but readers insist Petit Pierre at the bottom of the high drag-lift is the best on the hill.

More on the slopes

For beginners

Perfectly placed at the western end of the village, in the middle of the gentle home slopes, is a 150m covered carpet-lift.

The main slopes are sunny and treeless, getting steeper higher up; some of the lodgings are ski-in/plod-out

Then, to looker's right you have the 700m Valena fast (but slow-loading) chair-lift. And from that you can ski to the eastern end of the village to ride the 2km Valbiolo fast chair to ski the long, easy blue run down its length. These are excellent arrangements. Ideally, avoid late-season holidays when the sun might spoil the snow, and therefore your fun.

For true blue skiers

You'll open up a reasonable amount of skiing if you can make the step up to easy reds. If not, you're going to find the resort very limited.

If you're in serious need of confidence, you might like to ski down Tonalina, dropping only 275m over the course of almost 3km to the mid-station of the gondola link with Ponte di Legno. Otherwise, the place to head first is the blue Valbiolo on skier's left of the home slopes – a lovely run, much longer than the other blue pistes – approaching 3km.

After that, you're looking at easy reds. At the top of Valbiolo, Tonale Occidentale is one of the easiest, with the best snow in this sector (the clue is in the name – it faces east). Then it's worth heading over to skier's right of the home slopes, to Bleis and Giuliana, together offering a magnificent 5.5km of easy red.

For confident intermediates

Accepting the limited total extent, there's quite a lot to enjoy here. The reds on the two longer lifts directly above the village are OK for a warm-up, but the real interest lies elsewhere.

The top runs on extreme left and right of the home slopes are both good fun – Contrabbandieri is varied and scenic, Alpino delightfully secluded and a bit more challenging. You'll want to get up to the glacier for the views and the snow, even if the runs up there are nothing special. The black to the valley is very much at the easy end of the spectrum, and facing north it usually has good snow, so confident skiers should have no trouble with it; great fun on a good day.

To access the slopes of Ponte di Legno you have two options: ride the lower stage of the gondola to the main lift station, or ski the Pegrà red run to the slow Sozzine chair-lift. This delivers you to a choice of two black runs. Corno d'Aola is not seriously steep (in fact in the past it

was classified red), but the Variante has a steeper pitch.

All of Ponte di Legno is worth exploring, with the caveat that the relatively steep lower slopes may not have great snow. The lifts to plan on using for laps are the two high fast chairs, La Croce and Casola. Finish off your day with a run down the ridge from the top drag-lift on skier's right of the hill.

For experts

The black runs don't offer many challenges except in the snow conditions department in/after warm weather. Happily, there is a wide range of stuff to do off-piste, starting with easy areas near the pistes on the chair-lifts that stretch back into the hills above the village – Contrabbandieri and Bleis. But there is much more to it than that.

The piste map shows some of the area's classic off-piste runs. Vescasa (E) is a good warm-up run on skier's right of the main piste area over open slopes and light forest to the pass road. But there is much more to do in the high, shady Presena sector.

From the top of the first gondola you can branch to skier's left of the black piste to the valley to ski Alaska, or go to skier's right to descend the Alveo Presena route marked (C) on the map or, for more of a challenge, to find the classic Canale del Diavolo directly towards the village. From the next lift you can access seriously steep and exposed routes on skier's left of the lift system, often involving some mountaineering. For the rest of us, the must-do route is from the very top of the lift system – Sgualdrina Cantiere (B), down the huge bowl of Val Presena. There are lots of variants.

The big local adventures are day tours, starting by skiing off the back of the Presena area and then climbing to descend the long Val Narcanello (A) to the Ponte di Legno lifts at 1300m. You can climb 400m to the 2940m Passo di Pisgana to do the famous Pisganino run, or climb a further 200m to the 3150m Passo di Bédole for the Pisgana run – a vertical of 1850m.

Fancy stuff

The fair-sized Adamello snow park runs the length of the 700m Valena chair-lift on skier's left of the main slopes.

Passo Tonale – the resort

Passo Tonale has been developed to accommodate skiers, but not designed for their convenience. Broadly, it consists of chalet-style hotels lining the road approaching the nearby pass summit, and big but low-rise apartment residences set along a higher parallel street, plus an increasing number of small tower blocks dotted around. The place is rather dominated by cars, moving or parked, with pedestrians playing second fiddle.

Convenience

It's quite a compact village, under 1km long, with most of the lifts starting at the eastern end near the pass, and all the lodgings are a walkable distance from a lift. The place hasn't been designed for skiing to the door (it hasn't really been designed at all), but some lodgings offer it, discussed below.

Lodgings

The hotel scene is dominated by 3-star places, but there is a full range. The big, modern Paradiso, exclusive to Crystal Ski Holidays, is nominally a 5-star, in a great position at the foot of multiple pistes and lifts. There is a handful of 4-stars. In the past we've stayed happily in the 3-star Sporting, which is one of several hotels on the upper street that enjoy ski-in/plod-out locations. Our pick, though, would be the 3-star Torretta, closer to the main lifts and the core of the resort.

Out of the ordinary

The Faita, a little way down the hill towards Ponte di Legno, has five rooms with mezzanines on the top floor. Perhaps more exciting is the modern Capanna Presena, up at the glacier, with eight suites and probably the best view from a spa you have ever seen. Off-piste on skier's left of the home slopes the map shows a restaurant named Ospizio S Bartolomeo; this former monastery is now run as the hotel Mirandola, retaining many original features.

Bars and restaurants

At close of play there are several lively bars around the lift bases. The Baracca is a plate-glass box with a woody interior, usually with a DJ or a band; Magic Pub is more trad. Cantuccio and the Bait are relaxed places with good snacks. You can eat at many of these places, but top tips for dinner are Focolare and the hotel Torretta (great pizza, people say).

Off the slopes

Across the road from the main lifts is a natural ice rink. For swimming, it's down to Ponte di Legno. There is dog sledding, and snowmobiles can be hired. There are snowshoe routes up into the ski slopes, and many more down in the valley below Ponte di Legno. There are also cross-country trails down in the valley near Ponte di Legno, and more extensive trails near Vermiglio in the opposite direction.

For families

As so often, the key is to find the right lodgings – check out the hotel Torretta, in a great position on the snow. Near the ice rink is a kids' snow-tubing slope. There is a kids' teaching area with carpet-lifts, and an attached play area.

The Ponte di Legno option

Ponte di Legno is a proper little town with a life of its own and a summer tourist trade. The valley road bypasses the neat pedestrianised centre, which was virtually destroyed in WW1, and has at its heart a *ponte di legno* – a wooden bridge.

Hotels and restaurants are dotted around the spacious suburbs. There are four 4-star hotels, all rather distant from the lift station. The 3-star hotel Bleis is among the closest – about 200m away.

Staying down in Ponte di Legno makes little sense for the many novices attracted to this area – there is a moving-carpet slope at the lift station, but once you're off that there's nowhere to go. But it works for intermediates, who will want to spend some time on the Ponte di Legno slopes.

A key factor for some will be the leisure facilities. There is already a 25m swimming pool, and an ambitious new thermal spa is under construction, between the centre and the lift station, scheduled to open for 2021/22. A zipline is due to open for 2019/20.

A taste of what is to come in the Sella Ronda region: the 'hidden valley' run, easily reached from Alta Badia

Sella Ronda

Val Gardena (Selva, Plan de Gralba, Santa Cristina, Ortisei) /
Alta Badia (Corvara, Colfosco, San Cassiano, La Villa, Badia) /
Arabba / Val di Fassa (Canazei, Campitello, Alba and other areas)

Limitless piste skiing amid mind-blowing dramatic scenery

If you appreciate spectacular mountain scenery, and are happy
appreciating it while cruising on endless smooth pistes rather than
creaming through powder, you should consider a trip to the Sella Ronda.

The area is vast. From the top lifts at Ortisei to the lift base for
Marmolada, it's an astonishing 27km, as the eagle flies. At its core is a
unique circular tour – clockwise or anti-clockwise –around the massive
Gruppo del Sella, but most of the skiing available is actually off that circuit.
It's difficult to establish figures for the piste km of the whole area; but it's
clear that it's something like 400km – enough to rival the French Paradiski
area, but not the giant Trois Vallées. We have no hesitation at all in giving
this area Italy's only ★★★★★ size rating. All of this skiing, and more, is
covered by the amazing Dolomiti Superski lift pass.

The area offers a wide range of resort villages, neatly grouped at the
four corners of the piste circuit, all with additional slopes off the circuit.
Selva in Val Gardena and Corvara in Alta Badia at the two northern corners
are the most compelling, and we cover them in detail. Selva has the better
local slopes for competent skiers, but Corvara is better placed for outings
to Cortina and Arabba.

Arabba, at the south-east corner, has excellent, challenging local slopes
but also is the launch pad for the excursion on skis to glacial Marmolada,
the highest peak in the Dolomites. Val di Fassa, at the south-west corner,
offers several other ski areas within easy driving or bus-ride distance.

The snowfall in this south-east corner of the Alps is famously erratic;
it tends to be feast or famine. When we first visited San Cassiano [cough]
years ago, it was a time of famine, and we faced sunny pistes involving
what felt like as much walking as skiing; then a metre of snow arrived
overnight. These days, the snowmaking here is so widespread and so well
done that you can count on flawless pistes even in a prolonged drought.

Of course, snowmaking doesn't help off-piste, and there are other
factors that limit the area's appeal for freeriders. The Dolomite terrain is
different from the Alpine norm, and there are few high, open bowls. It's
also the case that there are restrictions on skiing off-piste, particularly
in the region of Veneto (which includes Arabba). These restrictions are
difficult to nail down, but they seem to revolve around the idea that off-
piste skiers can put piste skiers (and others) at risk of avalanche. Skiing off-
piste near/above pistes, particularly around Arabba, is asking for trouble –
though it is done, as you can see from the gondola mid-station in particular.

There are, however, lots of rewarding routes to ski in the area, including
some spectacular couloirs between sheer cliffs. We give an overview of
these routes in a single panel at the end of the chapter.

The Sella Ronda circuit

The circuit naturally gets busy, unpleasantly busy at times. We reckon it's worth doing, though, particularly if you can avoid the crowds by doing it on a Saturday or in low season.

You can ski the circuit either way, and there are colour-coded signs to help. Some resort piste maps include a sort of topographical map, but it's too cramped to be much use, especially at Selva. A clearer one is available from some lift stations and tourist offices.

The runs total about 23km, and the lift rides take two hours. In normal circumstances, expect the trip to take five to six hours, allowing for lunch — so with an early start there's time to explore some slopes off the circuit along the way.

People say the clockwise route is the more interesting but more crowded option. Now that the lifts from Corvara are much improved, we reckon the anti-clockwise route is just as appealing.

Sadly for true blue skiers, both routes involve a considerable amount of genuine red run skiing.

Perfect pistes surrounded by stunning scenery

Val Gardena – Selva

Selva / Plan de Gralba / Santa Cristina / Ortisei

Val Gardena is at the north-west corner of the Sella Ronda circuit and, in addition to the most varied and rewarding chunk of the circuit itself, offers a lot of local skiing – Seceda, accessed via Santa Cristina, and Alpe di Siusi, accessed via Ortisei, further down the valley.

If one or other of those areas is your prime target, staying in those resorts would make sense. For most of us, with plans to travel further afield, Selva makes more sense. It's a busy, attractive place with excellent nursery slopes, in a fabulous setting. It is rather spread-out, without much of a central focus, and traffic intrudes, but devotees forgive these flaws.

The mountains in brief

Size Vast. Read the Sella Ronda introduction
Slopes A good mix of gradients; some trees; some good long runs
Snow Unreliable snowfall, but hugely impressive snowmaking
System, Lift Ronda circuit queues aside, a quite slick system; some flaws
Sustenance An exceptional number of good restaurants
For beginners Excellent nursery slopes, but you have to travel to progress
For true blue skiers You're confined to two areas; the circuit involves reds
For the confident A great launchpad for skiing in all directions
For experts One of the better bases in the area; some big off-piste descents
Fancy stuff A decent main park, and several funslopes

Selva – the resort in brief

Convenience There are slopeside lodgings, but most require use of buses
Lodgings A very wide choice of middle-market hotels
Bars and restaurants Plenty of après action, and a good range of eateries
Off the slopes If sports are a priority, look at Ortisei rather than Selva
For families Choice of the right location is crucial

Pass notes	Key facts		Key ratings	
You save a bit by buying a local pass rather than a Dolomiti Superski pass, but trips to Corvara and Canazei are irresistible even if the full circuit doesn't tempt you. Beginners can buy a prepaid debit card to pay for lifts, costing €80.	Altitude	1570m	Size (see intro)	★★★★★
	Range (local)	1280–2520m	Snow	★★★★
	Slopes (see text)	400+km	Fast lifts	★★★★
			Mountain rest's	★★★★★
	Where to stay, ideally		Beginner	★★★★
	Above the centre, near the nursery slopes.		True blue	★★
			Confident	★★★★★
	Websites		Expert	★★★
	valgardena.it		Convenience	★★★
	There are several other, unofficial sites with similar addresses		Families	★★★
			Village charm	★★★

The mountains in detail

From the top of the extensive nursery slopes, the Dantercepies gondola goes off east towards Passo Sella for Corvara and the clockwise circuit. Closer to the middle of Selva, a gondola to Ciampinoi gets you going anticlockwise, southwards on a chain of lifts and runs below the impossibly dramatic Sasso Lungo, through the micro-resort of Plan de Gralba.

From Ciampinoi you can instead ski to Santa Cristina, where an underground train conveys you to the gondola for the Seceda sector. From there you can ski to Ortisei, with a gondola/cable-car for the return. On the other side of Ortisei, a gondola with no return piste accesses the vast Alpe di Siusi, also reachable from the much lower valley town of Siusi.

Size

The area is vast. Read the Sella Ronda introduction. Selva is well placed, with access to not one but two sectors of slopes away from the main circuit.

Slopes

Selva has lots of skiing to resort level, with a decent amount in the trees below the open upper slopes. Nursery slopes apart, the local slopes are all red or black, but there is easier skiing not far away at Plan de Gralba. Those local slopes offer vertical in the order of 700m, 800m if you descend to S Cristina. If you start from the slopes above Passo Sella you don't add much vertical, but you do add length – it's about 6km to the edge of Selva. The biggest descent – not just here, but in the whole Sella area – is the 1240m vertical from Seceda to Ortisei, a splendid run of about 7km.

Here, as in Val di Fassa, the pistes are not identified on the map – an irritant to us, and perhaps to you. On the other two Sella Ronda maps they are numbered.

Snow

You can be confident of good piste skiing although not of deep powder. Read the Sella Ronda introduction.

From the Dantercepies slopes: Sasso Lungo; the piste from Ciampinio; and distant, gentle Alpe di Suisi

System, Lift

In general the system is pretty slick. There are some non-crucial slow chairs in the middle of Alpe di Siusi (although one, Bamby, is being replaced by a fast six-seater as we write in 2019), and others dotted around on Seceda and elsewhere.

As noted elsewhere, the lifts involved in the Sella Ronda circuit get busy in high season. The lifts up to Seceda from Ortisei present a problem: the gondola from Ortisei shifts about twice as many per hour as the cable car above it. Queues result. One reader also recently encountered long queues for the Col Raiser gondola out of S Cristina.

At Ortisei, the two gondola stations are widely separated. Although a series of underground moving walkways link the Seceda gondola station to the town centre, you still face a 500m plod across the town to/from the Mont Seuc gondola.

A bus service not covered by the lift pass links Alpe di Siusi with Monte Pana/ Mont de Seura.

Sustenance

As you can see from our map, the number of mountain restaurants is extraordinary. But in fact there are many more than those shown – on Alpe di Suisi, about twice as many as the map shows. What's

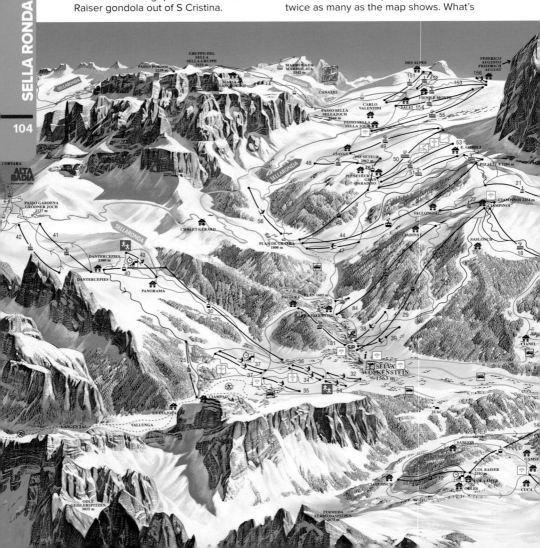

more, there are countless places with a lively atmosphere, good food, helpful staff and reasonable prices. We can mention only a few in the limited space we have.

On Dantercepies, Pastura and Panorama are tipped. In the Ciampinoi/ Plan de Gralba sector our favourite is Piz Seteur's relaxed, woody table-service restaurant on the upper floor, with some tables squeezed on to the small balcony. Rif Emilio Comici is a fashionable, busy place renowned for its seafood; beware: the terrace loses the sun quite early. The more down to earth Piz Sella gets rave reviews for its pizzas. Low down on the red piste to S Cristina, Cianel at the hotel

Pozzamanigoni gets good reports. For the slopes at Passo Sella, read the Val di Fassa section of this chapter.

On sunny Seceda, Baita Daniel is the reader favourite – lovely food and friendly service. Other recommendations include Gamsblut, Odles, Sofie, Curona and Pramulin, low down on the home run. On the lower part of the lovely long run to Ortisei, Costamula is outstanding – an ancient farm building, beautifully restored (with a small museum), doing superb food.

On Alpe di Siusi we have enjoyed good lunches at the cosy Baita Schgaguler Schwaige and at the gondola station, though it's more notable for

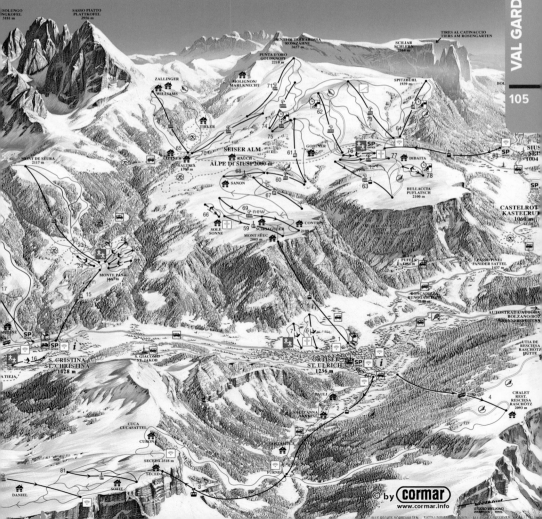

its fine view of Sasso Lungo than its ambience. Further afield, recent reader tips are Baita Spitzbühl and Laurinhütte, on the edge of the *alpe,* with great views. Earlier tips: Sanon, Dibaita and Zallinger.

More on the slopes

For beginners

The nursery slopes are excellent – long, broad, gentle, close to the village, slightly away from through traffic, sunny. Sadly, there are no longer runs immediately on hand to progress to – you have to take a bus up to Plan de Gralba, where there are excellent slopes. You pay for the beginner lifts by buying a points card.

For true blue skiers

Your options in the Val Gardena area, sadly, are confined to two areas.

Much the more rewarding is above Plan de Gralba, a bus-ride up the road towards Passo Sella. A bit of a plod up from the mid-station of the gondola brings you to a row of three fast chair-lifts serving a total of four blue runs of reasonable length – about 1km. The one on lift 50 has good snow (it's the shadiest) but has a steepish start and a narrow winding section; that apart, all are splendid problem-free blues.

The upper stage of the gondola takes you to a short, really easy linking run, stupidly classified red, to the top

of chair 48 and a good blue run down its length. At the bottom of this you can carry on down a lovely easy, scenic blue, about a mile long, to another nice blue piste served by drag-lift 56 – and so to the gondola base. In good conditions at a quiet time, you might then consider tackling the red run back to Selva – mainly gentle, with just one steepish bit.

The less rewarding place to head for is Alpe di Siusi. Here you face an awkward, narrow start to get to the quite testing blue served by chair 59, and your reward is an easier blue served by drag 66, all of 260m long; not a great package.

The really frustrating thing about Alpe di Siusi is that there is much more easy skiing to do, some of it classified blue, some red, but to get to it you have to deal with the start of the red run from chair 69, which is not easy. If you can hack that, you can roam widely over the area.

For confident intermediates

The red ink all over the map says it all, except that many of the red runs in the middle of Alpe di Suisi could be blue. For proper red skiing in that sector, you have to head for the high chairs on the far side.

There is excellent skiing from Dantercepies (the black as well as the splendid broad red), from Seceda (do not miss the lovely long run to Ortisei), all over Ciampinoi and on Piz Sella. The reds to Selva from Ciampinoi are pretty steep, and some who have hit hard or choppy

Selva has extensive, gentle nursery slopes (on the left) and a spectacular setting (that's Gruppo del Sella)

snow here, especially on the steep start of the sunny piste Ciampinoi 5, have not been happy. The blacks around Selva are mostly not seriously steep, and better snow on the blacks sometimes makes them easier – so Ciampinio 3 may be a better bet than 5. If you're enjoying good snow on the reds, you'll probably have a whale of time on the blacks.

The red and black runs on Mont de Seura are often neglected, and are worth a visit; the black piste is very easy.

If you go over to Corvara, on the way down take a few minutes out to ride the Frara gondola to Rif Jimmi. The gentle red back down is little used, and a great cruise in the morning sun.

For experts

If the snow is good the main satisfaction is skiing the easy blacks and tough reds on Ciampinoi without pausing for breath.

If the snow is chopped up or icy they become much more 'interesting'. The short black piste 5 from Piz Sella is steep at the start, and can be hard by the end of the day. The short black on Seceda is promoted as the steepest around, and in average gradient terms it is – it varies hardly at all, but is not notably steep.

When snow permits, there is off-piste scope outside the pistes from Ciampinoi toward Santa Cristina, and at the top of Dantercepies, and much more over at Seceda. Read the panel at the end of the chapter for info on more serious routes.

Fancy stuff

At Gran Paradiso above Plan de Gralba are a fair-sized terrain park and a family funslope, plus a boardercross course. And there are further funslopes on the drag-lifts above the nursery slopes, and above Santa Cristina on Ciampinoi.

Selva – the resort

Selva is a lively, traditional-style village set along the through-road leading to the other Sella resorts, and spreading up a sunny slope to its nursery lifts. It enjoys a spectacular setting in a position ideal for full exploration of the skiing; distance from Arabba and Marmolada is its main drawback.

Convenience

It's not a very convenient resort. There is very little slopeside accommodation. Depending on where you stay, you may be able to walk to the Ciampinoi gondola and to the nursery slopes to ride the drags up to the Dantercepies gondola – or to the Costabella chair-lift which accesses the Dantercepies red piste just above the gondola station. Ski buses run through the village and down to Ortisei; some run up to Plan de Gralba. Your lodgings may provide a pass; if not, it's €10 for a week. The service isn't great. The better hotels have their own shuttles.

Lodgings

The scores of hotels include almost 50 3-stars, almost 30 4-stars and a couple of 5-stars – the Granbaita is newly promoted; we've greatly enjoyed staying there. The 4-star Acadia, on the nursery slopes, gets good reports and is adults-only. Perfectly placed near the Dantercepies lift is the Continental, exclusive to the tour operator Inghams –

can't be faulted for its food or facilities, says a reader. Lower down in the heart of things are two 4-stars that readers love – the Posta al Cervo and the Oswald.
Out of the ordinary
Just on the Selva side of the pass is Passo Sella Dolomiti Mountain resort, a 4-star hotel with suites as well as rooms. On the road to Passo Gardena, Chalet Gerard is a cool, woody 4-star place with a fab view and good restaurant. You can stay at several mountain restaurants, including Piz Seteur – nine newly created rooms.

Bars and restaurants

Above Plan de Gralba, Piz Seteur is lively at teatime, whether you do or don't pick a day with dancing girls. Pra Valentini on the valley home run is a good place to celebrate your clockwise circuit. Then at the end of the piste there's the rustic Stua, with a DJ most days. For tea and cakes, head to Cafe Mozart. Later on, readers recommend Kronestube for traditional style, Goalies' Irish pub for music and beers, and Bar Oswald for great snacks. Luiskeller is a famously lively cellar bar.

There are plenty of good eating options, starting with the Stua above-mentioned. Nives serves more ambitious food in a charming panelled *stube*, or you can eat in its wine bar or cellar The Gourmet restaurant of the hotel Alpenroyal has a Michelin star, but the hotel Tyrol's Suinsom restaurant is widely regarded as the best in town.

Off the slopes

There's a hockey-size ice rink, with regular matches to watch. For tobogganing and swimming, look to Ortisei. There is lots of cross-country skiing in the area – in Vallunga, north of Selva, at Monte Pana and at Alpe di Siusi (with a connecting trail). The range of sunny footpaths and snowshoe trails is unrivalled – download the relevant topo map from the resort website.

For families

It's a pity you have to travel to Ortisei for swimming and proper tobogganing, but you can have fun on the huge nursery slope. Stay nearby for ready access to snow and you should have a fine time.

Alternatives to Selva

Up the road towards Passo Sella on the Ronda circuit, Plan de Gralba is a small collection of hotels. Two lift rides off the circuit, Santa Cristina is a quiet village with its own worthwhile slopes in the Seceda and Mont de Seura/Monte Pana sectors. Further down, Ortisei is the main town of Val Gardena, with lifts up to Seceda and Alpe di Siusi; good sports facilities.

Plan de Gralba 1800m

Blue run skiers wanting to hone their technique might want to consider staying in one of the handful of hotels at this isolated lift base, with a gondola to the best blue skiing in the area. The 3-star hotel Valpudra is well placed. Soochic is a cool restaurant with a very eclectic menu, including seafood.

Santa Cristina 1430m

Santa Cristina is a long, neatly traditional village, bypassed by the valley road to Selva, stretching almost 3km along the valley and spreading up the sunny side of it. The pistes and lifts are at the east end, where an underground railway links pistes and lifts on Ciampinio (above Selva) and Seceda (shared with Ortisei). There are nursery slopes up at Monte Pana, and in the village.

The Snowbar Ruacia at the bottom of the Saslong slope has music from mid-afternoon. La Posta, in a fine old house, is about the best restaurant. Maso Paratoni is a lovely old farmhouse above the village doing Ladin dishes (which you may or may not be keen on). There are plenty of 3-star and 4-star hotels; we like the look of the Almhotel Col Raiser, up on the Seceda slopes. There's a natural ice rink in the village, and cross-country skiing up at Monte Pana.

Ortisei 1240m

Ortisei is a busy little town, bypassed by the valley road, with lots of fine old stone buildings along its car-free main street and around the focal Piazza S Antonio, but not much ski resort atmosphere. There is an adequate nursery slope at valley level, a short walk or a tricky short ski from the gondola for Alpe di Siusi.

On the long run from Seceda, Baita Pauli and Val d'Anna are lively spots for a last drink. In the town there are plenty of bars and restaurants. Tubladel is a serious restaurant, and cosily beamed. Cascade, Sotriffer and Mauriz Keller are recommended by readers. Anna Stuben is a Michelin star restaurant in the hotel Gardena Grödnerhof. One of five 5-star places, this has a great location close to the Alpe di Siusi gondola and the town centre. 4-star hotels are plentiful, but outnumbered by 3-stars. There are lots of hotels up on Alpe di Siusi, reached by road from Siusi.

MarDolomit is a good aquatic centre with indoor and outdoor pools and a laned pool (your hotel may provide free access). There are six or seven lift-served toboggan runs, those on Resciesa an exceptional 6km long and served by a fast funicular railway. Heaven! Other facilities include a big outdoor skating rink and a tennis centre with a climbing wall.

Alta Badia – Corvara

Corvara / Colfosco / San Cassiano / La Villa / Badia

Alta Badia is at the north-east corner of the Sella Ronda circuit. Corvara is on the circuit, and also shares with San Cassiano and La Villa a lovely wide area of mainly gentle skiing east of the Sella massif. There is some steep stuff, but not as much as in Selva and Arabba.

Within Alta Badia, Corvara is the obvious place to stay for access to the greatest amount of skiing (including Selva and Arabba). It's a pleasant, relaxed village in a spectacular setting, with some excellent hotels – and parts of it are very convenient for skiing.

The Ladin culture is alive and well here, whereas in Val Gardena it seems a bit overwhelmed by German culture (or language, at least).

The mountains in brief

Size Vast. Read the Sella Ronda introduction

Slopes Generally gentle, partly wooded, with some decent long runs

Snow State-of-the-art snowmaking makes up for erratic local snowfall

System, Lift Pretty good, but not without its flaws, some in annoying spots

Sustenance A highlight – Alta Badia has a real reputation for good food

For beginners Excellent – good nursery slope and fab progression runs

For true blue skiers Lots to explore, but some challenges in key spots

For the confident Great cruising, but also plenty of challenges to be found

For experts Some epic off-piste routes, but there are better launchpads

Fancy stuff The park and funslope look OK – they're above San Cassiano

Corvara – the resort in brief

Convenience Some ski-in/out lodgings, but most people face some walking

Lodgings A good range, with some captivating hotels

Bars and restaurants All you need, from a throbbing bar to a Michelin star

Off the slopes A few options – including skating on a big indoor rink

For families A reasonable choice, if you pick your spot with care

Pass notes	Key facts		Key ratings	
You save a bit by buying a local pass rather than a Dolomiti Superski pass, but trips to Val Gardena and Arabba/Marmolada are irresistible even if the full circuit doesn't tempt you. Beginners can buy points cards to pay for lift rides.	Altitude	1550m	Size (see intro)	*****
	Range (local)	1325–2550m	Snow	****
	Slopes (see text)	400km+	Fast lifts	***
	Where to stay, ideally		Mountain rest's	*****
	If the budget will stand it, hotel la Perla, slopeside in Corvara.		Beginner	****
			True blue	****
			Confident	****
	Websites		Expert	***
	altabadia.org moviment.it		Convenience	***
			Families	****
			Village charm	***

The mountains in detail

Corvara has two lift bases, separated by the breadth of the village and the little river Chiesa. The major one, a few yards outside the village, is on the Sella Ronda circuit: gondolas from here will get you on your way south/clockwise to Passo Campolongo and Arabba, or west/anticlockwise to Passo Gardena and so to Selva in Val Gardena. Going that way you pass Colfosco, which has a small but interesting area off the circuit.

The minor base is at the top of the sloping village, right next to some of the best hotels: a gondola goes up to Col Alto, from which point you can explore the rolling blue-run territory spreading across to San Cassiano, and south towards Passo Campolongo and Arabba. This broad area lacks a name; its high point is Pralongiá (2157m), so we're adopting that name.

The steepest, shadiest slopes in that sector go down to La Villa, which also has its own Gardenaccia slopes across the valley, linked by a two-way horizontal chair to Badia. Buses run between here and Kronplatz — mainly of interest to skiers based at the much more limited Kronplatz.

Size

The area is vast. Read the Sella Ronda introduction. Corvara has access to a lot of worthwhile skiing off the main circuit, consisting mostly of blue runs with quite a few red/black exceptions.

Slopes

The local slopes are typical of the whole Sella Ronda area: there are some challenging runs through the woods at low level, but most of the terrain is gently rolling, with few trees.

You cover long distances here, and sometimes individual descents rack up several km, but in general the runs are short, and verticals limited. Descents like the 600+m verticals from Piz la Ila to La Villa or from Piz Boé to Corvara are exceptional. Start that descent to Corvara

with the black run from the Vallon chair going to 2550m (the high-point of the Sella Ronda slopes, although not part of the circuit) and you get the Sella Ronda's biggest on-piste vertical, 950m.

Snow

You can be confident of good piste skiing. Read the Sella Ronda introduction. Snowmaking covers about 90% of the pistes, including the long blue runs down to San Cassiano.

System, Lift

The lift system is adequate rather than hugely impressive. In two parts of the Pralongiá sector there are groups of slow chair-lifts. The ones at Cherz/Passo Campolongo are a particular irritant – the slow Vizza chair to Cherz

is a mile long. But there is a steady flow of improvements; as we write in 2019, a new six-seat chair-lift is replacing the drag lift on the the Stella Alpina slope in the Edelweiss sector above Colfosco, and a gondola is replacing the slow double chair to La Crusc above Badia.

The long chain of lifts to Passo Gardena on the anti-clockwise circuit has improved over the years, but still builds queues on high season afternoons. It concludes with two chairs where one ought to suffice – and one of the two is slow (although its capacity is OK if the seats are filled). We suspect territorial matters are at the root of all this.

We get few reports of other queues, except at ski school departure time in Corvara and San Cassiano.

Sustenance

While the whole Sella area is very well equipped with good restaurants, Alta Badia has gone out of its way to develop a culture of good food, building on the appeal of the excellent restaurants in the villages of Corvara and San Cassiano. There are countless good places on the hill, usually with great views, and ten of them take part in a scheme to offer reasonably priced dishes conceived by Michelin-star chefs, some local, others from elsewhere in Italy.

For a serious lunch in the Pralongiá sector our favourite is La Veranda, downstairs at Col Alt, at the top of the Col Alto gondola. The room is a bit plain but the view and food are great. We've also greatly enjoyed Las Vegas, which looks quite traditional from a distance but has a cool, crisp interior. Other recent tips in this sector from readers include Capanna Nera, I Tablà, La Utia, Punta Trieste, Utia de Bioch, Utia Bamby.

On the Passo Campolongo slopes, Crep de Munt is tipped, as is the higher Piz Boè Alpine Lounge, which has a slick self-service restaurant and a lounge bar as well as a proper restaurant.

On the slopes from Passo Sella towards Corvara your options are more limited, which is one reason why the woody, welcoming Rif Jimmi near the pass gets very crowded – but we have had good lunches here despite that. Lower down, in the backwater Edelweiss sector above Colfosco, the upstairs restaurant at the eponymous hut is tipped, as is the higher Rif Forcelles.

At mid-mountain on the Badia slopes, Rif Lee offers a sheltered terrace, excellent food and friendly service.

Most of Alta Badia consists of blue runs, partly wooded, with Dolomite peaks always in view

More on the slopes

For beginners

There is a good gentle nursery slope served by a drag-lift near the gondola station, only a short walk from the village. Then the Borest gondola accesses long easy runs on the Sodlisia chair-lift and the Plans gondola at Colfosco – perfect progression terrain. You can pay for the lifts using points cards.

For true blue skiers

The Pralongiá sector is a lovely playground for reasonably confident blue-run skiers, with gloriously long runs to Corvara and, particularly, to San Cassiano.

But dotted around the many blue pistes are some tough stretches. Unfortunately, one comes right at the start of your day if you ride the Col Alto gondola: the exit has a slightly intimidating start. It's not super-steep, but seriously apprehensive skiers would do well to spend some time, first of all, finding their ski legs on the runs at Colfosco mentioned above under 'For beginners'.

The runs in the Edelweiss sector above Colfosco are also pretty straightforward – but they face south, so snow conditions can be challenging after mid-winter.

We can't claim to have skied all the blues in the Pralongiá sector, but runs to be wary of include the ones from Cherz (particularly the one to Passo Campolongo).

The area's real problem, however, is the lower part of the long run 8 from Pralongiá to Corvara: part-way down, immediately below the bottom station of the Pralongiá 2 chair-lift, is a long steep stretch, exposed to the afternoon sun, which our specialist blue-run consultant chose to walk down. This is a crucial link towards Corvara (so it's busy, too), and your week is going to be badly affected if you can't hack it.

A less serious problem is that the piste across the top of the village to get back to the base station of the Col Alto gondola is narrow, and rather tricky when the snow is slushy. If you don't like it you can carry on down towards the main lift base and get to the village from that side.

For confident intermediates

Competent skiers who are unencumbered by less confident companions might incline to the view that Selva or Arabba would make a better base than Corvara, with more challenging skiing immediately on hand. But they might be wrong: Selva and Arabba are a long way apart, so staying in one makes it awkward to spend much time skiing the other; Corvara is quite well placed for both.

And the local skiing of Alta Badia is not to be sniffed at, either. You'll find rewarding red runs of reasonable length from Piz Boè to Corvara, and at San Cassiano, La Villa and Badia – plus shorter runs around Passo Campolongo, between Piz Sorega and Piz La Ila and above Colfosco. It's worth exploring the backwater areas, at Colfosco and Badia.

Most people would agree that the 'hidden valley' run, half-way to Cortina, is a must. Read the Cortina chapter.

Taken together, Corvara and its easily reached neighbours add up to a feast of fabulously scenic intermediate skiing.

For experts

Alta Badia's steep skiing HQ is La Villa. The Gran Risa piste, a famous World Cup giant slalom race course, is a long, shady, genuine black piste (touching a serious 35° they say). Ski it after a race if you want to test your edges. The next-door red Altin is worthwhile, too. Alta Badia's other black pistes, at Piz Boè and Edelweiss above Colfosco, are not as steep, and much shorter, but the first at least is worth a try. There are further challenges easily reached at Arabba and Selva.

It's not difficult to find opportunities to stray off-piste on the Pralongiá slopes. Read the panel at the end of the chapter for information on more serious off-piste routes.

Fancy stuff

Alta Badia seems to have invented a brand for its various terrain offerings – Moviment – and has even given them a website. The impressive main Snowpark Alta Badia is on the Ciampai chair-lift on Piz Sorega, above San Cassiano – 14 boxes, 10 rails, 17 kickers, they say. Not far away are a 900m family funslope and a 600m funcross course. A bit further away on the Pralongiá 2 chair is a 950m Kidsslope; sounds a bit like a funslope.

Corvara – the resort

Corvara is the compromise base for the Sella Ronda. It's bigger and more upmarket than Arabba, much quieter than Selva. It's mainly set along the road through to Arabba, which climbs gently to a little piazza at the top, with a few shops; it's not a notably entertaining place, but traditional and pleasantly spacious. There is also a separate suburb of continuing development on the sunny slope north of the main village. Corvara is well placed not only for skiing to Arabba and Selva, but also for trips by road to Cortina, or at least to the famous 'hidden valley' run, half-way there.

Convenience

Nowhere in the main part of the village is more than 500m from the main lift base, and in the upper half of the village you're also close to the Col Alto gondola. At the top of the sunny suburb you might be 1km away. Many hotels run shuttles to the lifts, and others organise shared bus services.

Lodgings

Most of the hotels are 3-stars, but there are quite a few 4-star places and one 5-star, the Sassongher. We fell long ago for the 4-star La Perla, at the top of the village near the Col Alto gondola station. It offers the perfect blend of comfort, caring service and informal ambience – with half-board food good enough to render its Michelin-starred restaurant redundant. The 4-star Posta Zirm next-door is highly recommended by readers – as is the 3-star Berghotel Ladinia. We and readers have also enjoyed the 4-star Col Alto, at the bottom of the village.

Out of the ordinary
Many of the mountain restaurants, particularly in the Pralongiá sector, have bedrooms. We like the look of Las Vegas Lodge, and Cherz.

Bars and restaurants

The resort offers quite a limited range of options, yet seems to cover all the bases. Skiing home from Pralongiá, Capanna Nera is popular for a last drink on the slopes; at the village, the piste goes past

Whichever way you turn in Corvara, there are spectacular towers and cliffs; on the right is Sassongher

L'Murin, a lively après bar; for something cooler, L'Got is not far away; later, for an aperitivo or a nightcap, there's the bar of hotel La Perla or the Iceberg at the hotel Col Alto; for a pizza, several places but notably the Taverna under the hotel Posta Zirm; for something fancier, the Adlerkeller; for a blowout, the Michelin starred Stua de Michil, at hotel la Perla.

hall. There are short cross-country trails between Corvara and Colfosco, and quite a serious set of trails at Armentarola, just outside San Cassiano. There are cleared paths in several directions, and guided snowshoe excursions. For tobogganing, look to San Cassiano. The pool at the hotel Posta Zirm is open to the public by reservation.

Off the slopes

The tourist office produces a useful brochure of non-skiing activities. There's a hockey-size ice rink, open longer hours on bad-weather days, and a tennis

For families

Like the other villages here, Corvara has a kids' snow-playground, this one at the main lift base. There are also other opportunities to play on snow elsewhere.

Alternatives to Corvara

Colfosco has great slopes for true-blue skiers, and quite a lot of lodgings close to the snow; it is on the Ronda circuit – the other alternatives are not. San Cassiano's layout is inconvenient, but for some it has the attraction of home runs easier than piste 8 to Corvara. La Villa, on the other hand, is for those who like a crisp black slope to end their day. Badia's location out, on a limb, has little appeal. All the villages are built in traditional style.

Colfosco 1645m

Colfosco is only a 1km horizontal gondola ride from Corvara. It spreads along the road to Selva, again for about 1km, and up and down the hillside. There are lots of simple guest-houses, but also a dozen hotels, 4-star and 3-star. A reader endorses the general view that the Stria is the best restaurant in town.

La Villa 1430m

La Villa is a bit bigger than the other villages, and busier. The charm factor is undermined by the road through to Corvara and Selva. It's a village of parts. The main parts, set along this road, are slightly separated by the two nursery slopes, one short and one long. There's also a sizeable suburb up the hill west of the centre, at the top of the longer slope. The gondola to Piz la lla starts at the southern end of the village, about a mile from the northern end. There's a good choice of 3-star and 4-star hotels. The 3-star Gran Risa is right next to the gondola station and gets good reports. Inghams has a chalet-hotel here.

There's a swimming pool. Between La Villa and Badia, the hotel Lech da Sampunt is set by a small lake where skating is offered when conditions permit.

San Cassiano 1545m

San Cassiano is a long village, bypassed by the road to Cortina, with the gondola to Piz Sorega just outside, at one end. The gondola serves Alta Badia's one proper toboggan run, winding through the woods to drop 460m over 3.5km. Most hotels have a minibus to take you to and from the Piz Sorega lift.

It's a quiet place, with a small car-free stretch of the main street near the pretty little church, and lodgings spreading up the sunny hillside. If it has any noisy bars, we haven't found them. The dozen 3-star hotels dominate, but there are plenty of other lodging options. The central Rosa Alpina is one of two 5-star hotels – a lovely welcoming place where dining options include the famous St Hubertus, with three Michelin stars. For simpler meals, La Sieia gets good reports. The hotel Störes has a climbing wall. There's a Ladin museum.

Badia 1325m

Badia is a little rustic village (with a Rococo church) surrounded by areas of development, mostly well away from the through-road. There are a dozen 3-star hotels, and plenty of simpler guest-houses.

Arabba

At the south-east corner of the Sella Ronda circuit, Arabba, is an isolated village; the only alternative base nearby is the even more isolated Passo Campolongo. It's the most limited of the four Sella Ronda resorts, with few amenities and hardly any shops. Its local slopes are the best in the Sella region for competent skiers, but very little for blue run skiers.

Arabba is the launch pad for the glacial slopes of Marmolada – worth it for views, and for one glorious red piste from 3269m. But the trip is easily done from Alta Badia or Val di Fassa , and is possible from Val Gardena.

The mountains

A big gondola and two cable cars serve the local slopes and get you on the way to Marmolada or to Passo Pordoi, with another gondola offering an alternative for the latter purpose. A cross-valley chair links these slopes to the Passo Campolongo side. This is very welcome – but the approach from Campolongo gets dangerously congested.

Size The area is vast. Read the Sella Ronda introduction.
Slopes Arabba sits at a point where the typical Dolomite arrangement of sheer sedimentary cliffs above gentle pastures gives way to steeper slopes on an intrusive ridge of volcanic rock. The slopes go to almost 2500m at the local high-point of Porta Vescovo, giving a vertical of 900m to the village. Because they are steep, the local runs are not notable for their length. The upper slopes are open, the lower slopes wooded.
Snow You can be confident of good piste skiing. Read the Sella Ronda intro.
System, Lift The lifts on the local slopes below Porta Vescovo are impressively powerful; a recent report speaks of negligible queues even over New Year. Heading for Corvara involves slow lifts in either direction out of Passo Campolongo. And the trip to Marmolada takes you back

Monte Cherz, above Passo Campolongo – red on the left, blue on the right which steepens uncomfortably

a bit, involving two slow double chairs to Passo Padon, with queues at the first, and then cable cars on Marmolada that build serious queues in good weather.

Sustenance This is probably the least well equipped sector of the Sella area, but you won't starve. A favourite is Rif Fodom at the bottom of the Passo Pordoi slopes – lively, woody and welcoming, with good food and service; head upstairs for table service in a calm atmosphere. One lift above Arabba, Rif Burz is a splendid modern take on the chalet theme with great views from its picture windows (and good food, reporters say). At Porto Vescovo there is a smart self-service place but also a pricey table-service restaurant, Viel dal Pan, which gets conflicting reports. The slick self-service Cesa da Fuoch at the gondola mid-station does a good job. On the way to Marmolada, Capanna Bill is a perennial favourite – cosy, friendly, good value.

More on the slopes

For beginners Next to the Burz chair-lift station, close to the village, are nursery slopes with three free moving carpet lifts. But then ... read the following section.

For true blue skiers There is easy skiing to be done, on the Burz chair and above the mid-station of the Porta Vescovo gondola, but it doesn't form much of a basis for a holiday. Go elsewhere.

For the confident There's splendid testing skiing on the slopes above the village. At the top, the red from Porta Vescovo is about as steep as a red can be, but it then mellows. The blacks are only just of black gradient. And there's quick access to some quite challenging stuff on the circuit, towards Corvara.

For experts As noted above, the black runs are not particularly challenging, but very rewarding nonetheless. This is Veneto, which means that off-piste is formally banned except on remote routes – but the slopes above the gondola mid-station get heavily skied. Your call. Read the panel at the end of the chapter, too.

Fancy stuff There is a funslope on the sunny side of Bec de Roces, served by the Pale chair-lift.

Arabba – the resort

Arabba is an attractive, spacious, traditional village set mainly below the Sella Ronda lift stations but also spreading up the valley above them, along the road up to Passo Pordoi and Val di Fassa.

Convenience The village measures about 1km end to end, with the lifts more or less in the middle – so the walks are mostly bearable. Some lodgings above the lift base can be reached (slightly off-piste) on skis when natural snow permits.

Lodgings 3-star hotels dominate, but the default choice has long been the 4-star Sporthotel, set between the two lift bases and highly recommended by readers. The more central 3-star Melita is also tipped.

Bars and restaurants Bar Peter is an Austrian-style après bar, also doing good food. Other eating options are adequate.

Off the slopes There is snowmobiling at Plan Boè – apparently the only such facility in the Sella area. There's no public pool, but some hotels open their pools to the public. As we write in 2019 the fate of the village ice rink is uncertain. Guided snowshoe walks are offered.

For families There is a ski kindergarten. If you stay close to the nursery slope you should be OK. But the appeal is limited.

Passo Campolongo

Passo Campolongo is the watershed between Arabba and Corvara, located a bit nearer Arabba. The lift station where the two systems meet is about 700m on the Corvara side. There are lodgings dotted along the roadside between the pass and the lift station, and on the way down to Arabba.

We greatly enjoyed staying at the hotel Boè, which was entirely remodelled and extended in 2018; very comfortable, with good rooms, charming service and excellent food, set beside the piste a little way above the lift station. Among the alternatives is Laguscei Dolomites Mountain Hotel, at the lift station.

Arabba in March 2019 – heavily dependent on artificial snow, but not entirely

Val di Fassa – Canazei

Canazei / Alba / Campitello / Pozza – and Catinaccio / Carezza

Canazei, Alba and Campitello are close neighbours in Val di Fassa, at the south-west corner of the Sella Ronda circuit; all have access lifts into the circuit, but only Canazei has a piste down to the village. From Alba you also have gondola access to the small but varied, challenging and refreshingly quiet Ciampac-Buffaure area, shared with Pozza di Fassa.

Across the valley from Pozza is a tiny area called Catinaccio (centred on the hill of Ciampedie), with lifts up from Pera and Vigo di Fassa. And a short drive up from Vigo brings you to Passo Costalunga, at one end of a bigger area, Carezza. We cover these areas at the end of the chapter.

Ski buses link all of these places, but they are not free – in 2020, €3 a day or €12 a week, less if buying from your hotel.

The mountains

The cable car from Campitello goes to Col Rodella, a small, high area of slopes from which you can ski over Passo Sella to Selva. The gondola from Canazei and cable car from Alba go to different points on Belvedere, a larger, high area of slopes around Passo Pordoi, from which you can ski down to Arabba. These two areas are linked by pistes and gondolas via Pian Frataces

in the intervening Val de Antermont, from which point a piste goes down to Canazei. From Alba, a gondola opposite the cable car goes up to Ciampac, at one end of a chain of lifts and runs going via Buffaure to the edge of Pozza di Fassa.

Size The area is vast. Read the Sella Ronda introduction. The Ciampac-Buffaure area reached from Alba is small but not negligible – 23km of pistes. It can be combined with an hour or two on the

© by Cormar

even smaller Catinaccio area via a linking bus from Pozza to Pera.

Slopes Practically all the local skiing is above the treeline, with just the link at Pian Frataces and the runs to the valley in trees. These descents offer 900m–1000m vertical, and the run from the top of the Col Rodella sector to Canazei is about 5km. The biggest descent is the run from Col de Valvacin at the top of Buffaure to Pozza – slightly over 1000m vertical, and about 7km if you take the red piste rather than the black. But most of the local skiing is on short runs of limited vertical.

Here, as in Val Gardena, the pistes are not identified on the map produced by Dolomiti Superski – an irritant to us, and perhaps to you. However, the the Val di Fassa lift company produces a different Skitour Panorama map giving the numbers, names and lengths of lifts, along with all sorts of other information (but no mountain restaurants are marked). Well worth picking up.

Snow You can be confident of good piste skiing. Read the Sella Ronda intro. The descent to Canazei gets a lot of sun, and is liable to closure. The black descent from Buffaure to Pozza is also too sunny to be reliable; the red is more shady.

System, Lift The system is not without its flaws. There are slow chair-lifts in all three slope sectors; those on Col Rodella and Belvedere are of no great consequence, but the three at the top of Buffaure are a bit of an irritant – particularly the 1km-long Col de Valvacin chair-lift.

The Sella Ronda access lifts from Val di Fassa have long been prone to non-trivial morning queues in high season, and the addition of a third lift in 2015 – the cable car from Alba – doesn't seem to have solved the problem. There are a lot of visitor beds in the valley (55,000, they say – three times the number in Val Gardena) so perhaps it's not surprising.

Sustenance The slopes are littered with restaurants. There are two notable places on Col Rodella: Rif Friedrich August, off the beaten track near the top, is cosily beamed, with historic photos on the walls, and cracking Kaiserschmarren (share one unless you are feeling mighty greedy). Fienile Monte is a very small, upscale satellite of the much bigger Rif Salei just down the hill; seriously good food, and seriously good wine. Low down on the Belvedere slopes, Ciampolin is said to be busy but welcoming, with good food (there is a cosy table service grill stube).

The easy red piste from Sella Brunech towards Buffaure – blissfully quiet on a fine morning in March 2019

More on the slopes

For beginners There are nursery slopes just outside the village – nicely secluded and gentle, but shaded in mid-winter – and at Ciampac above Alba. But where do you go next? Read on.

For true blue skiers There is only one blue run on the map that you might head for, served by the Toè gondola from Pecol, reachable by the main gondola from Canazei. Naturally, when we visited in 2019 we wanted to ski it; but the run was nowhere to be seen. The other Belvedere slopes are mostly gentle, but have steep stretches near the top that justify their red classification. Go elsewhere.

For the confident Disappointing. The Belvedere slopes, described above, are unsatisfactory for red-run skiers, too. The runs on the back of Belvedere are more rewarding, and less sunny. The black from the top of the Alba cable car at Col dei Rossi may touch black gradient, but is really an excellent tough red. The run to the valley is one of the best, when snow conditions and crowds don't spoil it. The runs at Col Rodella are genuine reds, but very short – except the excellent run to the valley (which joins the Belvedere one).

Although it's a bit skeletal, the Ciampac-Buffaure area is excellent for confident intermediates. The two high-points of Sella Brunech and Col de Valvacin (both at about 2400m) have good red slopes back towards mid-mountain and in the intervening valley. From mid-mountain at each end of the area there are excellent easy black runs to the valley level (the Alba one offering a bit more of a challenge); at the Pozza end there's also a long red, less sunny than the black, with a superb top half and a bearable cruise on the lower half.

For experts The most entertaining piste skiing is on the descents at the two opposite ends of Ciampac-Buffaure. You're well placed here for countless adventures off-piste on the Sella massif – read the panel at the end.

Fancy stuff In the middle of the Belvedere slopes is the main Dolomiti Familypark and Funslope, 500m long and 100m wide, with all kinds of features including a BigAirBag. On the Norei chair at Col Rodella there is a 500m 'funcross' course – the latest hybrid. On the Buffaure di Sotto chair above Pozza there's a 500m snowpark to suit experts and beginners – and a family fun line.

Canazei has spread a long way down the valley from the centre, on the left of this photo

Canazei – the resort

Canazei is the biggest resort in Val di Fassa – a lively, traditional village with an old core, spreading for a mile or so along the valley road and up the slope on the sunny side.

Convenience The gondola station is on the valley road, towards the eastern end of the village. If you're based toward the western end, you'll want to use the valley ski-buses mentioned in the introduction. If staying centrally you have the option of using the road train that circles the core of the village.

Lodgings The 3-star hotels outnumber 4-stars four to one. The very Italian 4-star Dolomiti Schloss hotel is an old reader favourite, just west of the centre. Right next to the gondola station, the 3-star hotel Pareda gets good reports. Crystal has two catered chalets here (in 2019).

Bars and restaurants There are plenty of noisy alternatives (eg Paradis, Rosengarden, Montanara) but we head for the Valentini wine bar at the end of the home run – a cosy vault run by knowledgeable, friendly people. El Cianton is a serious small restaurant with cool, wood and stone decor – about the best in town.

Off the slopes Dòloandes is a swanky new aquatic centre with a five-lane 25m pool, fun pool, kids' pool, flume, saltwater pool, hot tub. There are spa and fitness facilities attached. There is a natural ice rink, and a big indoor rink at Alba.

For families All in all, this doesn't seem an obvious choice for a young family.

Alternatives to Canazei

Alba is a small, scattered village only slightly separate from Canazei – their centres are only a mile apart. It has clear attractions – a decent cable car into the Sella Ronda circuit, and a gondola giving you the option of setting off in a different direction. Campitello lacks that option, and its cable car has to handle a much bigger visitor population, but it is a proper, attractive village. Pozza makes little sense as a base for the Ronda circuit.

Alba 1495m

Alba came late to the Sella Ronda party with the construction in 2015 of its cable car to the Belvedere area. The lift station is right next to the gondola for the Ciampac-Buffaure area (which replaced a cable car in 2017), at the up-valley end of the village, not far from the hamlet of Penia. There is an area of lodging developments near the lifts, but most of the hotels are dotted along the road up to those lifts.

The nearest thing to a centre is the junction of the valley road with a minor road to the parish church and an elevated suburb. We've stayed happily at the b&b hotel Fedaia, located at this central point, opposite the ski bus stop; it's an old place that has had a slightly funky makeover and has gained a small but smart spa, and now wants to be called Joy Hotel Fedaia. We had a good dinner at the popular El Resolè restaurant-pizzeria, over the road. Nearby is the local hockey-size ice rink.

Walks and cross-country skiing in Val di Fassa

Cross-country is big in Val di Fassa; a major race takes place along the valley in January, the Marcialonga – 70km from Moena up to Canazei and then back down to Cavalese. An excellent leaflet is produced by the tourist office with a map of the valley from Alba down to Moena and details of the ten trails of differing difficulty along the valley, with altitude profiles and all that.

Similarly there is a map of walking paths and snowshoe routes. The one we have details 27 routes, but some have been badly affected by the ferocious storm that passed through the lower valley at the end of October 2018, flattening vast areas of forest. The map states clearly that most of the paths are not machine-prepared, so conditions will depend on how much the path has been used since a snowfall.

Campitello 1410m

Campitello is a sizeable village bisected by both the valley road and the river Duron, with its centre more or less where the two cross. Nearby is a tight huddle of neatly modernised old houses which attracts summer visitors, and the place as a whole retains a pleasantly uncommercialised air. Lodgings are spread widely around the village, many between the centre and the station for the queue-prone cable car for Col Rodella 400m away. The 3-star hotels outnumber 4-stars, and there are plenty of simpler options.

The Co-op store in the centre is not in the same league as the one in Cortina, but is very useful. There is a small, sunny nursery slope with drag-lift and moving carpet close to the village.

Pozza di Fassa 1340m

Pozza is a spacious village on the valley floor, at the far end of the Ciampac-Buffaure ski area shared with Alba. Its centre is just off the main valley road and most of its numerous hotels and shops are set along the side road leading to the gondola station. Pozza also has its own little ski hill rising steeply above the village, Aloch. Just outside the village is a nursery slope, mid-way between Pera and Pozza. There is a natural ice rink.

There are mineral-rich thermal springs here, put to various uses; QC Terme Dolomiti seems to be the main spa complex. The Vidor camping resort also has swimming pools. The prominent name on our map, Sèn Jan di Fassa, is the recently formed municipality containinig Pozza and Vigo.

Catinaccio

This is a scenic but low and very small area (the pistes add up to only 14km) reached by cable car from the top of Vigo di Fassa or by chair-lift from a roadside car park at Pera. There's a ski bus link from Pozza di Fassa, so you can reach it from Alba by skiing the Ciampac-Buffaure area. The area takes its name from the dramatic adjacent massif, better known as Rosengarten; the low peak at the core of the skiing is Ciampedie.

Ciampedie is a neat little hill. There's an extensive beginner area and kids' snow garden at the top; a sunny red run taking a long roundabout route down a summer road to Vigo; and varied slopes on the opposite, shady side – a lovely genuine blue with a rather narrow start, a genuine red and a genuine short black (Alberto Tomba) with one short section that is seriously steep. There is also a second blue that is a bit tricky where it merges with the red. A recent burst of investment means that the main chair-lifts are all fast – only the beginner lift at the top is slow.

There are half a dozen huts on the hill, none of them marked on the map.

Vigo di Fassa 1330m

Vigo is a pleasant village, its centre a mile from the centre of Pozza, though their suburbs are separated by little more than a stream. It is slightly elevated above the valley floor, with the cable car to Ciampedie on the upper fringe. There are plenty of hotels and guest-houses. The mountain and the deserted Val de Vajolet behind it are well known for snowshoe expeditions.

Pera di Fassa 1320m

The brand-new Pera chair-lift base accessing Catinaccio sits on the valley road between two hamlets which make up Pera di Fassa, the line of the lift neatly bisecting the space between their two rival churches. Across the valley is a nursery slope, mid-way between Pera and Pozza. Both components have lodgings within walking distance of the lift. In the centre of the southern part is the historic and highly traditional Albergo Rizzi, with guest registers going back to the late 19th century.

Carezza

This is another scenic area, but more extensive and going a bit higher than Catinaccio. It has a rather skeletal lift/piste system stretching about 6km from Passo Costalunga at the east end of the area via the resort of Carezza to Nova Levante at the west end.

Carezza, claiming 42km of pistes, occupies the right half of the small piste map we've reproduced on the previous spread. As you can probably see, it's essentially a simple system of blue runs down four linking lifts forming a chain across the lower slopes, plus some red runs higher up. All of the piste classifications are correct, and for blue run skiers there is a nice sense of travel on those four pistes down the lifts. The piste down lift 404 in particular is a lovely long run. That lift also serves a quite impressive snowpark, 700m long with medium, easy and family fun lines.

For more confident skiers, though, these runs don't offer much variety. Red run skiers will find the area a bit limited unless they can hack the three red pistes that have genuine black top sections; these sections (some quite long) get afternoon sun, so early in the day can be very tricky. Ignore the long red run at the bottom of the map down to Nova Levante – it is certainly long, but it's just a tedious get-you-home run down an enclosed valley. At Passo Costalunga there is a short (550m) wide black run of consistent black steepness on chair 414; good snow.

The lift system is quite slick; the two remaining slow chairs are set to be replaced in 2020. There is a grand plan to build a long cable car to the slopes from the village of Tiers, off to the north-west. Don't hold your breath.

There are about 20 mountain restaurants – staggering, for a small area. They are not marked on the piste map.

There's a gentle toboggan run down the lift linking the resort of Carezza to Pass Costalunga.

Passo Costalunga 1750m

This is a tiny collection of lodgings and car parks at the low pass. There is a beginner slope and kids' snow garden.

Carezza 1620m

Carezza consistly mainly of a large chalet suburb (without much sign of an urb) ranged up the gentle slope beside the Golf 1 chair-lift – yes, it goes over a golf course. There is a short beginner slope at the lift base, and another across the hill at Moseralm, where the eponymous 4-star hotel looks a good bet for a comfortable ski-in.ski-out stay, although rivalled by the Sporthotel Alpenrose at the main Carezza lift base.

Nova Levante 1180m

Nova Levante is a small village spread along narrow wooded valleys at the bottom of the long Laurin gondola, but big enough, probably, to be the main resort of this area. There is a beginner slope and a kids' snow garden at the top of the gondola – but no longer blue runs to progress to. Start at one of the other bases.

Websites

fassa.com
valdifassalift.it
carrezza.it

catinacciodolomiti.it
fassaski.com (not official, but useful)

Off-piste routes around the Sella Ronda

From most points of view the precipitous Gruppo del Sella looks unskiable, but in fact it offers couloirs in all directions. Guiding outfits list 20 or more recognised routes. And there are worthwhile routes elsewhere, too. As always, go with a guide, properly equipped.

Most of the Sella Ronda runs are reached from the one lift that goes seriously high on the massif, the cable car from Passo Pordoi to 2945m on Sass Pordoi. Some involve little or no hiking, including Val Lasties, one of the easiest descents, on the south-west aspect of the massif (starting down the shady Valon del Fos), and the south-facing Forcella Pordoi, joining the line of the cable car; the stiffer Canale Joel involves a bit of a climb.

The most conspicuous and the most famous Sella run, seen in our photo from the Edelweiss sector above Colfosco, is the broad Val Mesdi. This spectacular descent about 4km long starts near Piz Boè, the high-point of the massif, and involves an hour's skiing, walking and climbing from the cable car. Other well known routes include short, steep and narrow Val Setus, west of Val Mesdi.

On the east side of Sella, the Vallon double chair above Passo Campolongo goes to a worthwhile 2550m and accesses routes to left and right.

Higher Marmolada also has a wide range of excellent runs, long and shady, most skied directly from the two upper cable car stations without any hiking, many presenting no great difficulties. The popularity of the cable cars with piste skiers can limit your laps, though.

The Padon ridge separating Arabba from Marmolada has some good routes, including a bunch from Passo Padon (2370m) mostly going north-west, notably the classic Valle Ornella. From Forcella Europa at the top of the gondola out of Arabba there are descents north and south. The latter used to deliver you to an ancient bucket lift for runs on the lower slopes of Marmolada, but sadly it reached its use-by date in September 2019.

At Passo Pordoi, a short hike south-east from the Belvedere lifts accesses a long, sunny, easy run to the Alba cable car station.

On the dramatic Sasso Lungo above Passo Sella there are several routes but they all require a lot of climbing. Back in the day, the ancient gondola to Forcella Sassolungo (now closed in winter) served a short but serious black piste. The run is scarcely worth climbing for, whereas the 'north' route (actually going north-west) is a lovely long run to the Monte Pana lifts (with some plodding towards the end).

At Passo Gardena there's rather less climbing to reach the ridge above the deserted Val Chedul, for a lovely run west to the Selva lifts. Down the valley, another serious climb from the top lift of the Edelweiss sector takes you to Forcella di Ciampei, point of departure of two very different runs. One is down Val Culea into another long valley leading to Selva, Vallunga. The other is the local cult descent, Valscura, a long, straight, narrow couloir, said to be less extreme than it looks from below (or from Piz la Ila above San Casssiano).

On the rolling hills between Corvara and Arabba there are easy routes from some of the high-points, notably Pralongia and Cherz.

Val Mesdi seen from Colfosco's Edelweiss sector

Mid-mountain above Falcade, Passo San Pellegrino area; in the distance, the slopes of Civetta and M Pelmo

Southern Dolomites

Latemar / Passo San Pellegrino / San Martino di Castrozza / Civetta

A quick look at four little-known but worthwhile ski areas

The huge Dolimiti Superski region is dominated by the Sella Ronda circuit and the offshoots at its four corners, which gets its own huge chapter just ahead of this one. Leave the Sella Ronda circuit at Canazei, at the south-west corner, and you're in Val di Fassa, which we cover in that long chapter. But Val di Fassa is also a gateway to several other ski areas worth exploring, and there are quite a few other areas in the southern Dolomites reached in other ways. None of them are well known internationally. In this chapter we're covering briefly the four areas most worth knowing about.

Carry on down Val di Fassa, and it becomes Val di Fiemme. To the west of the valley, Ski Center Latemar links Predazzo to Obereggen. To the east, up a side valley from Moena – the largest commune in Val di Fassa, and a charming little town – another area links the pass-top hamlet of Passo San Pellegrino to the lower village of Falcade. South from there, the road through the very limited slopes of Passo Rolle leads to a third area, above San Martino di Castrozza. And off to the east of Falcade is a fourth area, Civetta, linking three valleys you've probably not heard of.

South of Moena is the smaller area of Alpe Lusia, going over to the slightly elevated side-valley village of Bellamonte. We've tagged this on the end of the San Pellegrino section.

5 Val di Fassa (Sella Ronda)	9 San Martino di Castrozza
6 Arabba (Sella Ronda)	11 San Pellegrino / Alpe Lusia
8 Ski Center Latemar	12 Civetta

Ski Center Latemar

Predazzo (Val di Fiemme) / Pampeago /Obereggen

The name we've used for this area, little known in Britain, isn't universally used locally, either – you'll also see the area called Val di Fiemme-Obereggen, or suchlike. The name is taken from the Gruppo del Latemar, which rises in typically Dolomite fashion from its slopes.

The mountains

Val di Fiemme, downstream of Val di Fassa (at one corner of the Sella Ronda area), is at one end of the area, with a gondola into the slopes from the fringes of Predazzo, a valley town. The hamlet of Obereggen is at the other extremity. In the middle of the area is Pampeago, too small to be called a hamlet, at quite high altitude.

The three resorts are linked over several ridges and bowls. In the Val di Fiemme, the skiing doesn't go below mid-mountain – you ride the gondola down. They claim 49km of pistes, which in any case puts the area in our ✳ size category. But checking some of the resort's published lengths for individual runs shows that the usual exaggeration is going on. So it's a small area, but it offers variety and a sense of travel – Obereggen is over 6km as the eagle flies from the lifts at Predazzo.

The heart of the area, from the top of the Obereggen gondola to the high runs above Pampeago, suits both blue- and red-run skiers. Where there is blue skiing

there is usually red skiing not far away, so a mixed group can stay in touch. The green runs on the map are footpaths.

On the fringes of the area, though, there is a notable absence of blue. The skiing above Obereggen is all red (but blue-run skiers returning from the central slopes can ride the gondola down). At the Predazzo end there is nothing for blue-run skiers to do – but there are some black runs, as there is on lift 27, to looker's left of Pampeago. All of these blacks offer some proper black stretches.

At Obereggen there is a good snow park, which includes a quite serious half-pipe, even.

It's a modern lift system. As we write in 2019, one of two slow chair irritants – lift 21 in the valley to looker's right of Obereggen – is being replaced by a very powerful eight-seater, leaving only lift 42, high above Pampeago, to annoy you. The only other slow chairs are on beginner slopes at mid-mountain above Predazzo and Pampeago.

As usual in the Dolomites, the slopes are littered with restaurants. Check out the cutting-edge Oberholz, for a start.

The resorts

A feature of the area is the enthusiasm for toboggan runs, a rare thing in Italy.

At mid-mountain above Predazzo is a sled-on-rails coaster and a proper toboggan run served by a chair-lift. At Pampeago there is a toboggan run down the Campo Scuola chair-lift. At Obereggen there are two runs, one 50m long and one 2.5km long served by the gondola, open and floodlit three evenings per week.

Predazzo 1020m

Predazzo is a neat little town on the flat valley floor with an ancient core of narrow cobbled streets. This is the place to learn more about what makes the Dolomites such distinctive mountains, at the town's geological museum.

The gondola into the skiing starts a mile from the centre; there is a ski-bus service. The nursery slope and kids' snow garden are at mid-mountain. Like the higher Val di Fassa, Val di Fiemme is big on cross-country skiing, with various options nearby. There's a 25m laned swimming pool, with small training pool, hot tub and gym. Hotels are plentiful, mainly 3-stars.

Pampeago 1760m

Pampeago is the ultimate micro-resort: two hotels, a few small apartment blocks, three ski shops, three coffee bars and a ski school. All set in a prettily wooded, remote valley, with a car park serving the two chair-lifts.

In summer the road beyond the lift station over Passo Pampeago has often formed part of the Giro d'Italia cycle race.

Obereggen 1550m

Obereggen is a bit more substantial than Pampeago – the hotel count runs into double figures, just. But that's about all there is to it, apart from the ski shops of course. It's more remote from centres of population than Pampeago, so actually gives more of a sense of seclusion. The hotels are arranged up a sunny slope above the lift station, with the beginner slope running down beside them. For a quiet holiday away from it all, this place takes some beating.

More information

latemar.it
visitfiemme.it
eggental.com
visittrentino.info

First tracks above Pampeago – out of sight, below the trees on the left, probably still in the shade

Passo San Pellegrino

Passo San Pellegrino / Falcade

No, it has nothing to do with mineral water – the watery San Pellegrino is some way west, above Bergamo. This San Pellegrino is a pass on the road east from Moena (in Val di Fassa) to the village of Falcade, with skiing around the pass and down to that village.

Tourism bodies like to lump the little neighbouring area of Alpe Lusia (in the right half of our map) together with Passo San Pellegrino in an imaginary thing they call the Tre Valli carousel. Our map contrives the impression that their pistes almost touch, but in fact they are miles apart.

The mountains

There are two slope sectors: open slopes on the sunny side of the pass at 1918m, going up to almost 2400m, and more varied slopes on the south side of the pass, starting with a cable car to Col Margherita at 2513m. The two add up to 67km of pistes, they say.

The skiing on the sunny side of the pass is served by two fast quad chair-lifts a mile long supplemented by drags and slow chairs, including a double chair at the top to the high point of the sector. Essentially, one of the big chairs serves blue pistes, and the other serves red.

A piste crosses the road to the station for the cable car to Col Margherita. It's not clear from the map, but from there you can ski in two widely separate directions to Falcade – to skier's left, red runs

leading to a black stretch in the woods, or to skier's right, a red run leading to the 6km-long Innamorati blue run around the back of Laresei (helpfully not named on the map). This meets the aforementioned black for a final red descent to Falcade. A gondola from Falcade takes you first to the mid-mountain area of Le Buse.

For competent skiers the Col Margherita sector has lots to do, accepting the limits of its small size. To make the most of it you do need to be able to hack the easy black stretch on the way to Falcade. For blue-run skiers, it is hopeless. With an average gradient of 10%, Innamorati will not entertain red-run skiers, but the reds that top and tail it have stretches that true blues won't like.

The black runs here generally justify their classification, and the area has built a bit of a reputation for off-piste. There are some serious although quite short

routes to do on the shady side of the pass from the cable car, and the lift company and its associates operate a scheme called Col Margherita Freeride Park to help people get into off-piste safely by managing an avalanche-protected mountainside, with controlled access. Sounds like an excellent initiative.

There are beginner slopes and kids' snow gardens at the pass, and at mid-mountain above Falcade, accessed by gondola.

Sanpe Snowpark is served by the 500m Campigol quad, but is said to be 800m long; there are four lines, including one for beginners.

There are mountain restaurants at key points, with a cluster above Falcade.

The resorts

We imagine most people will ski this area on day trips from Val di Fassa. Moena is only 10km down the hill.

Passo San Pellegrino 1918m

PSP is nothing more than a string of lift stations dotted along the pass road, on either side of the summit, with a handful of hotels and associated ski shops (and a neat little church) occupying the spaces in between. We can see only one good reason to stay up here: fresh tracks after a dump. There are cross-country trails of all standards to the west of the pass.

Falcade 1150m

Falcade is a spacious village which spreads along its wooded valley from the gondola station for 2.5km. It has a few hotels; the 4-star Molino is a low-rise chalet perfectly positioned at the lift base.

Alpe Lusia

This is a resort-free area, accessed by gondolas starting at Ronchi (1370m), 2km outside the lovely old valley town of Moena, and a point 200m higher on the back of the hill, 2km from the small mountain village of Bellamonte. The area claims 27km of pistes.

The Moena side is shady and steep, with genuine black runs top to bottom and good red alternatives at the top. Apart from steeper stuff on chair 205 (which is much longer than it looks on the map), the sunny side is mostly easy, with a lovely top-to-bottom blue about 5km long. Ironically, the one beginner slope and nearby snow garden are on the steep side. On the sunny side there is a snow park – and a toboggan run.

More information

fassa.com
passosanpellegrino.it
skiareasanpellegrino.it
dolomiti.org/en/falcade
visittrentino.info

Descending from Col Margherita; ahead, the minor mound of Laresei; beyond, the peaks above Passo Rolle

San Martino di Castrozza

San Martino has a famously scenic setting beneath the Dolomite spires of the Pale di San Martino. It's a quite smart little resort, with a limited but interesting ski area, and further high slopes a few miles up the road at Passo Rolle.

The mountains

The skiing is in two quite different sectors – a single slope from Col Verde served by a gondola starting on the upper fringe of the sloping village, and a big horseshoe chain of runs and chair-lifts over several ridges and valleys west of the resort, accessed by gondolas at opposite ends of the horseshoe, both about 1km from the centre. The small sector has a cable car above it that serves a serious off-piste run.

In the main sector, the two lift systems meet at the area high point on the shoulder of Cima Tognola, at 2343m (not to be confused with the slightly lower Alpe Tognola). From there you can make lovely long descents of up to 6km and 900m vertical to the valley stations. They say the pistes (including Passo Rolle) amount to 60km. We're unconvinced by this claim: evidence from elsewhere and our own limited measurements suggest the total is well under 50km. So it's a small area, getting a ✳ size rating. There's a nice mix of wooded and open slopes.

The slopes suit confident intermediates best, with plenty to do within the obvious constraints of the area's small size. For the less confident there is a lovely long blue run down the length of the Colbricon access gondola, and a higher area of slopes on Alpe Tognola, but from there you need the gondola to return to the base.

The two short black runs barely deserve the classification, but there is a lot of good off-piste potential. As well as the obvious departures from the pistes, the Scandola bowl between the two peaks of Cima Tognola and Alpe Tognola beckons; the descent of wooded Val Cigolera, in the middle of the area, is a local classic; and then there is the steep 670m vertical run down the cable car from the shoulder of Rosetta.

There are beginner slopes next to the village and at Alpe Tognola.

There's a sunny snow park 1km long on the Tognola lift, with three lines and a Burton Progression Park.

After a long dormant period, the lift system is now steadily improving, with a gondola replacing two slow chairs from

© by **cormar**

the valley in 2018 and a six-seat fast chair (12) replacing the Cigolera drag on the upper slopes in 2019. Next for replacement is the double chair to Cima Tognola from the Alpe Tognola sector, but this will still leave some double chairs. Snowmaking covers 90% of the slopes.

The mountain restaurants are not numerous here, but you won't starve.

The local cross-country trails amount to 30km.

The resort

San Martino is a long-established resort, with some big, grand hotels dating from its reconstruction after WWI. It is still quite fashionable, drawing a lot of weekend business from the Venice area.

The village is set on a slope, the top about 100m higher than the bottom. Most of the hotels, shops and restaurants are set along the through road to Passo Rolle. This levels off in the centre, where there is a little neat pedestrian zone near the tiny church. It's all pleasant enough, but the big hotels are obtrusive.

There's a skating rink next to the sports centre, which has a tennis court.

There are five 4-star hotels, and countless 3-stars. There are isolated lodgings near the lift bases, but it's best to stay in the centre and use the ski-bus (which also serves Passo Rolle).

Ranch is a famous Western-themed bar. For a different vibe: La Mia Enoteca.

Passo Rolle

Passo Rolle is a high, open area centred on a road pass at 1984m; it's a 9km drive from San Martino, but less than half that distance as the eagle flies – back in the day there was a chair-lift link, and there is still hope of reviving it. It has little appeal as a place to stay, but there are two or three simple hotels.

The slopes have something for everyone, including a genuine black piste, but the lifts are short – only the one serving the red runs at the top of the map approaches 1km – and they are all slow. The piste map shows no trees, but in fact the slopes on the San Martino side of the road are wooded. There's a Railz Park on the long chair, 800m long.

More information

sanmartino.com
tognola.it
visittrentino.info

San Martino enjoys a fabulous setting; just visible on the skyline, we hope, is the Rosetta cable car

Civetta

Alleghe / Santa Fosca / Val di Zoldo

This area, south of Cortina's Cinque Torri area, consists really of two lift networks a mile apart but with blue pistes across the gap in both directions. The lifts up Marmolada, more usually reached on skis from Arabba, are only 15km from Alleghe, and a ski-bus will take you there.

The mountains

In the larger, northern half of the area, two chains of lifts and runs form alternative routes between the lakeside village of Alleghe and Santa Fosca, in Val Fiorentina. Blue runs link this to the southern area, as does a road over Passo Staulanza (1766m) to Palafavera, one of three lift bases here; the others are slightly lower down in Val di Zoldo – Pecol and Pianaz. Lifts and runs form a horseshoe above these two lift bases.

Strangely, the piste map shows practically all of the northern sector as treeless, when actually it is largely (and pleasantly) wooded, to one degree or another.

The area claims to be Veneto's biggest; Cortina might have something to say about that, but Cortina's slopes are fragmented. They claim 80km of pistes. Christoph Schrahe's more realistic figure is 57km, and another independent source puts it at only 51km. Anyway, it looks like a ✳ size rating. But for a small area it gives a good sense of travel, measuring an impressive 8km from end to end. Snowmaking is comprehensive.

One of the chains of lifts from Alleghe to Santa Fosca is all fast lifts, but the other involves three drags. The lift out of Pecol is a gondola, and at altitude there is a mile-long fast chair, but the other lifts in this sector are slow – from Pianaz, access is by a drag followed by a double chair.

For once, the amount of blue on the map does not deceive – you can get around most of the area on blue runs. But, as you can see, there is no blue skiing above Pianaz and the final descents to Alleghe and Pescul are red. There's just about as much red skiing as blue, so it would work well for a mixed party.

There are black pistes dotted about; they are steep only in short stretches – run 37 down chair 35 has a steep section, run 6 a very steep pitch. There is plenty of opportunity to head off-piste within the lift system, and some established routes outside it – from Monte Fertazza to Alleghe, for example.

At mid-mountain above Alleghe there's a beginner slope and kids' snow garden, and a snow park.

Mountain restaurants are no more than adequate in number. As you might hope, Belvedere at the top of Fertazza does enjoy a fabulous view.

The resorts

The name you'll see used most often alongside Alleghe and Val di Zoldo is Selva di Cadore. That's the comune the whole Val Fiorentina belongs to, but Santa Fosca is the main village in the valley, and close to the lift station door at the outpost of Pescul – Selva is two miles away.

Alleghe 980m

Alleghe is a pleasant little resort in a picture-postcard lakeside setting. It has nine 3-star hotels and a couple of 4-stars. The gondola station is at lake level, and the village is on quite a steep slope.

There's cross-country skiing nearby. Amazingly, there's a hockey-size ice rink.

Santa Fosca 1410m

The lift station is at Pescul, a hamlet only a few yards from the rustic village of Santa Fosca. There are lodgings here, but much more choice in the larger village, where there is also a nursery slope, kids' snow garden and an ice rink. There's cross-country skiing further up the valley.

Val di Zoldo 1390m

Pecol has been developed for skiing in a low-key way – lots of chalets dotted around a pleasant central area with a church. It has an ice rink. There are several hotels. Mareson, just down the valley, is a delightful old rustic village.

The nursery slope and kids' snow garden are at the top of the gondola. There's cross-country skiing between the lift bases, and up at Palafavera.

More information

skicivetta.com
dolomiti.org

Spectacular Monte Pelmo, seen from the red Cristelin piste from Pian del Crep to Pecol, in Val di Zoldo

Via Lattea

Sauze d'Oulx / Jouvenceaux / Sestriere / Pragelato / Sansicario / Cesana Torinese / Claviere + Montgenèvre (France)

Extensive area marred by a poor link towards France

The core of this area, from the Italian point of view, is a lift network resembling a three-pointed star centred on Monte Fraiteve, with old favourite Sauze d'Oulx forming one point, and the others being Sestriere and Sansicario. The last is connected rather tenuously to slopes above Claviere which spreads over the French border to Montgenèvre.

Thankfully, the days are long gone when Sauze was famous chiefly as the favoured resort of young impecunious Brits bent on overindulgence of various kinds, and it is now a much more balanced resort.

Like Passo Tonale, Sestriere displays the Italian talent for building high resorts to accommodate skiers without bothering to design them for skiers' convenience. To be frank, we don't really see the point.

To make the most of the whole Via Lattea, if you don't require evening diversions, there's a case for staying in Sansicario, a modern micro-resort.

A warning

Early in 2019 the red and blue pistes from Monte Fraiteve towards Sauze were closed, following the tragic death of a child skiing one of them. Those unable to hack the two easy black pistes, 25 and Colò, had to take buses or taxis to go from Sestriere and Sansicario to Sauze. For many people, the available skiing was effectively halved. As we go to press in September 2019 it is not clear when normal service will be resumed. Given that a fatal accident above Claviere in 2016 resulted in lift and piste closures lasting three years or more, the outlook is rather grim.

Sauze d'Oulx

There's a lot to like about Sauze d'Oulx – an animated village with a positively charming core; friendly and fairly extensive local slopes with bits of woodland; long views into France; very large amounts of additional skiing on hand in the connected resorts.

But the resort needs more investment. It's eight years since the last fast chair-lift was installed, and the three adjacent chairs (below, above and to skier's right of it) are all slow – the last, Cote Faure, installed only in 2017. Across the mountain, both the chairs involved in the link with other resorts are slow. The return from Sansicario is via a pair of parallel drags.

All of which the resort's many devotees cheerfully overlook. 'A friendly, welcoming resort,' says a regular. 'Easy to fall for,' says a recent convert.

The mountains in brief

`Size` A big area in Italy, and a decent additional area accessible in France

`Slopes` A good variety of gradient and a mix of wooded and open slopes

`Snow` A weakness: a flaky snowfall record, and incomplete snowmaking

`System, Lift` Another weakness, with far too many slow chair-lifts remaining

`Sustenance` An adequate choice, and one or two gems

`For beginners` There are many better places to start

`For true blue skiers` The key is to step up to skiing easy red runs

`For the confident` A great area, given good snow

`For experts` Pray for powder, and pay for guidance

`Fancy stuff` They say there will be a park at Sportinia

Sauze d'Oulx – the resort in brief

`Convenience` Pick your spot with some care

`Lodgings` Something for everyone, including the budget-conscious

`Bars and restaurants` Animated, no longer rowdy; some decent restaurants

`Off the slopes` A weakness: no swimming, skating or tobogganing

`For families` Not an obvious candidate for a family trip

Pass notes
A pass covering the whole Via Lattea is available, but it is quite a bit more expensive than the pass for just the Italian side. It's not clear whether a daily upgrade will be available in future. Beginners can buy special day passes covering just a few lifts.

Key facts
Altitude	1450–1550m
Range	1370–2789m
Slopes (see text)	270km

Where to stay, ideally
Close to the Clotes chair-lift.

Websites
vialattea.it
sauzedoulx.net
turismotorino.org

Key ratings
Size	****
Snow	**
Fast lifts	***
Mountain rest's	***
Beginner	**
True blue	***
Confident	*****
Expert	***
Convenience	**
Families	**
Village charm	****

The mountains in detail

The home slopes split into two unequal halves, both reachable by riding the slow Clotes chair-lift followed by the fast Lago Nero. The area where most people spend most of their time is to looker's right of the lift, centred on the mid-mountain micro-resort of Sportinia – a clearing in the woods, with hotels as well as restaurants and a carpet-lift. This is usually accessed by the Sportinia fast quad starting an irritating distance from the village centre. On looker's left of Lago Nero is an area of red runs served by two drags and the recently installed Cote Faure chair-lift. Absurdly, this area will be open in 2020 only at weekends and at Carnival time.

Above Sportinia, another chair gets you on the way to the Colò chair up to Monte Fraiteve. From here, runs served by drags at the top and chairs lower down descend a west-facing slope to Sansicario, and the link to Claviere and eventually Montgenèvre.

Alternatively, from M Fraiteve you can take either of two pistes down to the mid-station of the gondola from Sestriere. Here there are two hills linked only at resort level – M Sises, directly above the village, and M Motta, equipped with two long, fast chair-lifts and supplementary drags.

Size

Now that the link from Montgenèvre is fully open again, we think it's fair to focus on the whole Via Lattea including the French sector. The usual claim for this area is 400km of piste. As usual, we don't believe this figure – it would put the area on a par with the Paradiski area in France, and we're confident it's nowhere near that big. The resorts don't publish individual run lengths, but Christoph Schrahe comes to the rescue with his published figure of 269km (just ahead of Cervinia-Zermatt). So it rates ✳✳✳✳ for size.

Sauze has a pleasant mix of lightly wooded and open slopes; M Fraiteve is the meeting point with Sestriere

Slopes

At both Sauze and Sestriere the skiing is on open slopes at the top, descending into woods. Because Sauze is lower than Sestriere there is much more skiing below the treeline here – it's a great place to be in a storm. The mountainside above Sauze is basically of easy red gradient; the mountains at Sestriere are more varied, with some genuine steep stuff.

A lot of the runs on the upper slopes are quite short, but runs to Sauze and Jouvenceaux can be quite long – approaching 1300m vertical, and 8km long. The chair-lift from Jouvenceaux rises almost 800m to Sportinia.

At Sestriere, M Motta delivers much more vertical than M Sises – as well as peaking 200m higher, it has a lift base 200m lower. Of more practical interest is that the Nuova Nube chair on M Motta

has a vertical of 700m. Three black pistes are designated as mogul slopes.

Snow

The Italian side of the Via Lattea has a rather erratic snowfall record and at times relies heavily on snowmaking, which has improved over the years but is still not comprehensive. The main slopes face north-west, so are reasonably shady, but the Sansicario runs get the afternoon sun, and suffer accordingly. These and other low runs may be closed for lack of snow, which these days is not what you expect. You hardly ever hit a closed piste in the Dolomites, for example. So snow is not a strong point.

Heavy snowfalls do happen, of course. But there were reports in 2019, in particular, of the resort taking too long to get runs groomed and open after a fall.

System, Lift

As we've said in the introduction to Sauze, the resort's lift system is seriously flawed once you depart from the fast-lift axis above and below Sportinia. Despite this, queues seem to be a problem only on sunny weekends.

Particular irritants are that the more convenient of the two lifts out of the village, the Clotes chair, is slow (although not very long), and that the lift to M Fraiteve is a slow double chair shifting only 1200 people per hour. It is supplemented by a rather tricky drag.

At Sestriere, the picture is a bit brighter – normally, the only concern is the drag-lifts at the fringes of the system accessing black runs. When the wind blows and the higher lifts close, everything changes: the burden then falls on slow chairs on the lower slopes of both hills. Not surprisingly, queues then result.

M Fraiteve is accessed from Sestriere by a gondola, operating at a typical gondola speed. But many people ride it down, especially when snow conditions on the very sunny slopes to Sestriere are poor, and its quite modest capacity is then not up to the job.

Sustenance

The piste map supplied to reproduce here does not have restaurants marked, but the printed one we have on file does.

Widely acknowledged to be the best on the mountain at Sauze is Ciaô Pais, a small hotel tucked away in the woods off the 2000 piste – lovely food and friendly, kind staff. Further down the hill is another small hotel, the upscale Capricorno; we've enjoyed its restaurant, Naskira, but it now seems to get mixed reports.

Naturally, there's a bunch of places at Sportinia, including some doing table service. We've enjoyed meals at Rocco Nere. Capanna Kind is strongly tipped for service, food and value. On the Sansicario slopes the best bet is Baita Mavie, near the top of the Sellette chair-lift. On our agenda is Grange Tachier on run 12.

At Sestriere, an experienced reader tips two self-service places: the woody little Raggio di Sole, near the top of the Pragelato cable car, for good food, good music and a nice vibe; and Chisonetto, a stone and wood chalet on the Bimbo blue run, for its lovely buzzy atmosphere, excellent food and great value.

More on the slopes

For beginners

There is a slope near the Clotes chair-lift station in the village equipped with a carpet-lift, but it is meant to help skiers reach the chair – it is too steep for beginners, who are expected to schlep out to the Sportinia chair-lift to go up to the long carpet-lift at Sportinia. The chair-lift is fast, which means it is very slow when loading, but even so this is far from the ideal way to start skiing. If you must come to the Via Lattea, consider staying over the hill in Sestriere. Once you are ready to move on, you can tackle a reasonably gentle blue run above Sportinia, accessed by the Rocco Nere fast chair. There is a special pass covering just the lifts you need.

For true blue skiers

How well you'll get on in Sauze depends crucially on taking the mental hurdle of skiing easy reds. Until you take that step your access to the easy blue skiing at the top of the slopes will depend on riding the Sportinia chair back to the resort at the end of the day: all the pistes from mid-mountain are red. Life isn't made any easier by a piste map that is seriously difficult to follow.

The easiest way down is to start on piste 11 and then pick up piste 29, being sure to take the easier variants to the right. You end up on the blue slopes on the Clotes chair-lift out of the village – but many runs converge here so these slopes are very busy at the end of the day. Once you have cracked 29 and maybe 11, the door is open to try the lovely piste 12 to Jouvenceaux and Gran Pista to Sauze.

The run above Sportinia on the Rocco Nere fast chair is an obvious early target. From that lift you can progress to the open bowl below M Fraiteve, with the option of doing laps on the slow Chamonier chair or taking the Colò chair to the peak, for access to Sestriere. There are blue runs to Sestriere; but the one from the mid-station of the gondola does not offer much rewarding skiing, and both runs are very sunny, and may be icy or slushy even when other slopes are not. Take local advice about their condition.

At Sestriere your main target is the chair-lifts on M Motta, accessing two blues. Bimbo from mid-mountain is mostly gentle; it has a stiffer stretch in the middle, but at least that part is wide. Piste 68 is a fine run at the top but follows a road lower down (you can switch to ski Bimbo instead).

For confident intermediates

If the snow is good and everything is open, this is a great area for the confident skier, with some fine, long although mainly rather flattering reds, and easy blacks to call on when you feel the need for the occasional challenge.

All the more direct runs above Sauze and Jouvenceaux are worthwhile, but be sure also to devote some time to cruising the Moncrons sector (if it's open). It's not at all direct, but run 12 to Jouvenceaux is delightful if the snow is good (parts get a lot of sun), with a gladed area halfway down. If the snow above Sansicario is surviving the afternoon sun, the runs here are excellent, particularly red 71 down to the gondola mid-station and the black Olimpica, the women's downhill race course, which in many resorts would be classified red.

The approach to Claviere, just down the road from Montgenèvre but on the Italian side of the border

Another French connection – Montgenèvre

The Via Lattea (or Milky Way) mainly consists of Italian resorts – Sauze d'Oulx, Sestriere and Sansicario, plus Claviere on the French border – but also includes Claviere's close French neighbour, Montgenèvre. The border area offers varied slopes and good snow (thanks to its location on a pass), and experts can have a fine time off-piste here; but its appeal for piste-bashers is much reduced by the many slow lifts.

The Via Lattea has never quite realised its potential, largely because the link from the main Italian resorts through valley-bottom Cesana Torinese to Claviere is a bit of a turn-off. To reach the effective start of the border area skiing at Colle Bercia from the bottom of

the Sansicario pistes you have to ride a gondola down and a chain of three chair-lifts up – one fast (but a mile long) and two slow. Even then, you're still some way from the Montgenèvre slopes.

Recently other problems have arisen, with some important lifts and pistes at altitude on the Italian side of the border closed from 2016 to 2018 following a fatal accident on a piste. These closures meant that for three seasons you could access Italy from France only by plodding along a flat piste at resort level. Happily, in 2019 the key Italian piste from Colletto Verde was re-opened, restoring the high-altitude link. The Col Saurel chair-lift at the head of the valley and its long red run have also been brought back to life.

Most of the red runs on M Motta at Sestriere offer more of a challenge combined with good vertical, but you'll need to look to the easy blacks for anything seriously testing – read the 'For experts' section.

For experts

The only black pistes of any significance at Sauze are those from the top and the shoulder of M Fraiteve; neither is a genuine black, which was just as well during the piste closure crisis (mentioned in the introduction) that put the red and blue alternatives out of action for most of the season in 2019. As we've said above, the much longer black Olimpica piste on the Sansicario side of the hill is also more of a tough red in practice.

Many of the black runs at Sestriere are also at the easy end of the spectrum – for example, KN (Kandahar Nisa) on M Motta is a lovely cruise when the snow is good. But the three ungroomed runs served by high drag-lifts – at the top of M Sises and M Motta, and on looker's left of M Motta – are genuine blacks (and of course usually mogulled). Piste 2, the most direct of the groomed runs on the lower part of M Sises, is also a proper black.

There are good opportunities for skiing between the pistes all over the area, at Sauze and Sestriere. We're told that throughout Piedmont it is now illegal to ski outside defined pistes without full avalanche kit.

This is not an area with a lot of major recognised off-piste routes, but there are exceptions. The Malafosse run to Jouvenceaux from the bottom of the bowl on the Sauze side of M Fraiteve, a black piste in the past, is now off-piste. And from the same starting point, when snow permits, there is the well-known Rio Nero run down to Amazas on the road from Oulx to Cesana – 1500m vertical if you start from M Fraiteve.

On skier's right of the lift network you can explore slopes that were lift-served in the past, above the hamlet of Richardette. In the opposite direction, there are descents on the back of the hill to Pragelato.

There are great off-piste opportunities over the border at snowy Montgenèvre.

Fancy stuff

The resort is planning to have a comprehensive snow park operating in the Sportinia area for the 2019/20 season, but they don't sound super-sure. There's one at Sestriere, too.

The village is no beauty, but it doesn't intrude too much into views from the slopes; this is the Clotes lift base

Sauze d'Oulx – the resort

Sauze enjoys a balcony setting, facing the mountains on the French border. It is neither a great beauty nor a great eyesore – its apartment blocks are on a human scale, at least – but has an appealing feel. Next to the lively central Piazza Assietta is the original village of narrow cobbled streets lined by old stone houses (and a lovely little church).

Convenience

Sauze is set on a steepish slope, and can be hazardous if the streets are icy. The Clotes chair-lift station is about 30m vertical above the old centre, the Sportinia lift another 20m higher. It's not a big place – although there are widely spread suburbs of small apartment blocks, most of the village would fit into a circle 700m across. The lifts are on the edge of that circle; there are lodgings close to the Clotes lift base, but many people face long walks. There are ski-buses running on three lines, but the service is poor, and cost €8.50 for a week pass in 2019. The better hotels have shuttles.

Lodgings

The roost is ruled by 3-star hotels, with quite a few 2-stars and three 4-star places (plus one on the mountain). For convenience, you won't beat the well-run 3-star hotel Stella Alpina. Only a few steps further away is another attractive option, the 3-star hotel Sauze. In the old village there are some simple but stylish B&B places, the pick of which are Gran Trun and Chalet Faure (with a small spa, and a lively wine bar in the basement).
Out of the ordinary
The Capricorno, in a charming spot beside the piste, is a 4-star hotel and the most expensive in the resort. The 2-star Ciaô Pais a bit higher up is more our style.

Bars and restaurants

There are plenty of places to pause for a last drink on the way home – the Sosta at Clotes is a good one – but for something a bit livelier head for Sportinia, where Capanna Kind often has live music.

In the village, over recent years many of the more notorious bars have closed (eg Paddy McGinty's, Cotton Club) while more civilised enterprises have sprung up. Our regular annual reporter tips Miravallino, Assietta, and long happy hours at Max Bar and Scacco Matto (with a big sun terrace). The Grotta has long been known for its cheap beer.

There are plenty of restaurants, mainly offering good-value, simple meals. The most highly regarded are the Ortiche, in a crisply furnished wood-lined room, and the Cantun del Barbaruc, in a vaulted old stable in the old village.

Off the slopes

There is not a lot to do. There is a sports hall with fitness facilities, but no sign of swimming or skating, and no proper toboggan run. There are several identified walks across the mountainside, classified for difficulty but not necessarily prepared.

For families

There's a baby fun park, and the bottom of the Clotes slope is good for sledging, complete with carpet-lift during the skiing day, at least. But on the whole it's not very enticing for young families.

Just down the hill

Jouvenceaux 1370m

The terraced suburbs of Sauze reach almost all the way down to Jouvenceaux, set on a steep part of the hillside, about 150m below the centre. On one side of the winding road is the cute old village, and on the other a broad area of low-rise apartment developments. The 3-star hotel Fontaine is handy for the lift. The hotel Martin is 300m away, across the road to Sauze, but has built up a loyal following. The 3-star hotel Etoile des Neiges and next-door rustic restaurant in the old village get enthusiastic reviews. The Bar Jouvenceaux on the roadside (just over the road from the Martin) is something of an institution – a tiny pub-as-a-hub shop/cafe/bar/restaurant that gets rave reviews for its snacks and super-filling fixed-price meals. The bright lights of Sauze are said to be a pulse-raising 25-minute walk away.

Sestriere 2030m

They say Sestriere was the first resort purpose-built for skiing (by Gianni Agnelli, of Fiat fame), so it's perhaps no surprise that it has flaws. It's high – 500m higher than Sauze – so it's nice and cold; but it's set on a pass, and when the south-west wind blows – or, worse, the north-east wind – it can be a bit Arctic. Like other early ski stations, Sestriere is not pretty; but Agnelli's main slip-up was that it's not conveniently laid out for skiing.

Its slopes offer more challenge than Sauze's, but Sestriere is also much better for beginners. And it's better placed for outings to France.

Beginners have carpet-lifts and drag-lifts on gentle slopes in front of the village, and a longer blue run to the satellite micro-resort of Borgata to progress to. **Convenience** It's not huge – leaving aside some of the peripheral residences, it fits into a circle 600m across. The lifts are all on the south-east side of the village, so you could be 600m from the lift you want. There are no pistes through the village – so there are buses, not free. **Lodgings** There are almost 20 hotels, mostly 3-star but with several 4-stars. The 4-star Cristallo has a great position close to the snow, as does Crystal Ski's hotel du Col. The Savoy Edelweiss is about the best-placed 3-star.

Bars and restaurants It's rather quiet during the week, livelier at weekends. Black Pepper is a lively bar. Pinky is a cafe-style bar that's perennially popular with Brits – good pizza. There are plenty of restaurants. Last Tango is a reader favourite. The Centro is noted for steaks. In the satellite of Borgata, Antica Spelonca is a lovely vaulted cellar. **Off the slopes** There's quite a bit to do. There's a sports centre with pool, an ice rink, good dog sledding, snowmobiling. There are cross-country trails here and more down at Pragelato. **For families** There's plenty of snow to play on, if you're based near it. There is a snow park on skier's left of the slopes.

The village of Sestriere sits below M Sises, on the right, but most of the skiing is on M Motta, on the left

Other alternatives to Sauze d'Oulx

The alternatives offer a wide range of differing attractions. The border village of Claviere is best thought of as a way of skiing French Montgenèvre on the cheap – it's only a mile or so away. Sansicario or Cesana might suit someone who wanted to split their time equally between Italy and France. Pragelato's USP is its big Club Med 'village'.

Claviere 1760m

Even more than Montgenèvre, Claviere was improved in the noughties by the removal of through-traffic to a bypass – it is now a positively pleasant place to spend time in.

There is a nursery slope right next to the village, and almost equally close are two chair-lifts – one to the Italian slopes and the other to Col Boeuf for runs in either direction.

There are several modest hotels – a wider choice than in Montgenèvre, in fact. The 4-star hotel Bes is a classic old-fashioned Italian hotel in a very central position. Popular bar-restaurants include the Gran Bouc and the Kilt.

Sansicario 1700m

Sansicario is a quiet, modern ski station in a sunny location, consisting mainly of low-rise apartment residences spread around the hillside below a fast quad chair accessing the red runs above the village and a short beginners' chair-lift (plus a kids' snow garden with carpet-lift) on a separate slope at the bottom of run 21. This is a good area for beginners and near-beginners, and there is also a longer blue run from the village to the mid-station of the gondola from Cesana. But after that all the skiing here is red.

The hotel Rio Envers now seems to be filled by British school parties, but the Majestic, some way down the hill, is still a regular 4-star. There are a couple of bar-restaurants. The Enoteca wine bar gets good reports.

Cesana Torinese 1350m

Cesana is a neat valley-bottom town at the junction where the valley road from Oulx forks left for Sestriere and right for Montgenèvre. The valley stations of the lifts linking Sansicario and Claviere are 800m from the centre. There are several hotels, mainly 2-star and 3-star, plus the 4-star Edelweiss.

Pragelato 1600m

In a sheltered valley 400m lower than Sestriere, with a cable car up and a blue piste down, Pragelato is mainly of interest to cross-country skiers – it hosted the races (and ski-jumping events) in the Turin Olympics – as well as Club Med devotees. This 'village' does, for once, resemble a village, with accommodation in lots of individual chalets. There is a carpet-lift on a beginner slope.
Website pragelatoturismo.it

Published in the United Kingdom by
Guide Editors

Editor **Chris Gill**
Consultant editor **Dave Watts**
Editorial assistant **Mandy Crook**
Design and production **Graham Wells**
Ad manager **Dave Ashmore**

Printed in England
by Pureprint Group Limited

ISBN-13: 978-1-9997708-1-5
A CIP catalogue entry for this book is
available from the British Library.

Trade orders to:
Central Books Ltd
50 Freshwater Road, Chadwell Heath,
London RM8 1RX
020 8326 5696
contactus@centralbooks.com

This first edition published 2019

Enquiries and feedback to:
publisher@wheretoski.uk

Photo credits/copyright

Resort index / directory

This is both an index to the resorts covered in the body of the book and a quick guide to other resorts you might consider for a quick visit. There are, of course, scores of smaller resorts in the Italian mountains.

Page references are to the start of the relevant chapter; minor resorts are generally covered towards the end of the chapter.

Abetone
Main resort in the exposed Apennines, less than two hours from Florence and Pisa – so makes a good short break option. Small and charming village, with prettily wooded slopes that are mostly north-facing and well-covered by snowmaking. There is some good intermediate terrain and excellent nursery slopes, three terrain parks and children's area. But most lifts are slow chairs and drags.
Alagna – Monterosa – 81
Small rustic resort on the east fringe of the Monterosa area.
Alba – Sella Ronda – 99
Virtually a suburb of Canazei, with lifts into the Sella Ronda and an area shared with Pozza di Fassa.
Alleghe – Southern Dolomites – 126
Lakeside village, the main resort in the quite extensive Civetta ski area.
Alpe Cimbra
Fair-sized ski area above Folgaria, south of Trento.
Alta Badia – Sella Ronda – 99
One of the main resort bases in the Sella Ronda area, containing Corvara and other resorts.
Alta Valtellina – 16
Region embracing Bormio, Livigno and other resorts.
Andalo
Sizeable resort in Trentino – a pleasant enough place with a small local town feel, at the foot of the fair-sized Paganella Ski area shared with Fai della Paganella. A gondola goes up from near the centre of Andalo and another leaves from a big car park nearby. The runs are mainly genuinely challenging reds and can be long; most are northish-facing and so keep their snow in good condition.
Antagnod – Monterosa – 81
Small village and ski area a few km down the valley from Champoluc.

Aosta – Pila – 88
Historic working valley town with a gondola up to the mountain resort of Pila.
Aprica
Straggling village between Lake Como and the Brenta Dolomites, with a fair-sized ski area accessed by lifts dotted along the road at the foot of the slopes. Popular with school groups.
Arabba – Sella Ronda – 99
One of the main resort bases in the Sella Ronda area.
Artesina
Purpose-built resort in the maritime Alps south of Turin. Part of Mondolè ski area with Prato Nevoso.
Badia – Sella Ronda – 99
Village out on a limb of the Alta Badia area.
Bardonecchia – 28
Bormio – Alta Valtellina – 16
Bressanone
Italian name for Brixen.
Brixen
Sizeable valley town with two worthwhile ski areas within reach – Plose and Gitschberg. Bressanone is the German name.
Bruneck – Kronplatz – 61
Town close to Reischach gondola base for Kronplatz area. Italian name is Brunico.
Brunico – Kronplatz – 61
Italian name for Bruneck.
Brusson
Major cross-country village in the Monterosa area, near Antagnod.
Campitello – Sella Ronda – 99
Sizeable resort in Val di Fassa, with a lift into the Sella Ronda.
Campodolcino – Madesimo – 67
Valley town with funicular up to Madesimo's slopes.
Canazei – Sella Ronda – 99
One of the main resort bases in the Sella Ronda area, in Val di Fassa.
Carezza – Sella Ronda – 99
Small ski area and resort off Val di Fassa, linking Passo Costalunga and Nova Levante (not linked to Sella Ronda).
Catinaccio – Sella Ronda – 99
Small, scenic ski area above Vigo di Fassa – not linked to Sella Ronda.
Cavalese
Major town in Val di Fiemme with worthwhile ski area at Alpe Cermis, reached by gondola. Ski Center Latemar also within reach.
Cervinia – 33
Cesana Torinese – Via Lattea – 136
Little village in the valley between the Sauze d'Oulx / Sestriere / Sansicario side of the Milky Way and the Clavière / Montgenèvre side on the French border.

Champoluc – Monterosa – 81
The most attractive base in the Monterosa ski area.

Cima Piazzi – Alta Valtellina – 16
Small but worthwhile ski area above Isolaccia, near Bormio.

Civetta – Southern Dolomites – 126
Quite extensive area in the Dolomites linking Alleghe, Santa Fosca and Val di Zoldo.

Claviere – Via Lattea – 136
Small village on the French border, linked to Montgenèvre (in France) and the rest of the Milky Way ski area.

Colfosco – Sella Ronda – 99
Minor village in the Alta Badia area.

Cortina d'Ampezzo – 41

Corvara – Sella Ronda – 99
The best-placed resort in the Alta Badia area.

Courmayeur – 49

Dolonne – Courmayeur – 49
Suburb of Courmayeur with a gondola into the slopes.

Entrèves – Courmayeur – 49
Unremarkable cluster of hotels at the base of a cable car up to Courmayeur's slopes.

Espace San Bernardo – 54
Extensive ski area shared by La Thuile and La Rosière in France.

Fai della Paganella
Trentino village at the foot of the fair-sized Paganella Ski area shared with Andalo. A chair-lift goes up from a big car park nearby. The runs are mainly genuinely challenging reds and can be long; most are northish-facing and so keep their snow in good condition.

Falcade – Southern Dolomites – 126
Veneto village south of the Sella Ronda with lifts up to slopes around Passo San Pellegrino.

Folgaria
Widely spread village south of Trento, at the foot of Alpe Cimbra ski area.

Folgarida – Madonna di Campiglio – 72
Small, traditional-style station, linked to Madonna di Campiglio's extensive area.

Foppolo
Modern, quite high ski station near Bergamo with a fair-sized area of slopes.

Frabosa Soprana
Small resort in the maritime Alps south of Turin, sharing the Mondolè Ski area with Prato Nevoso and Artesina.

Gitschberg
One of two worthwhile little areas within reach of Brixen/Bressanone (the other being Plose).

Gressoney-la-Trinité – Monterosa – 81
Smaller and higher of the two main villages in the central valley of the Monterosa ski area.

Gressoney-St-Jean – Monterosa – 81
Larger village down the valley from Gressoney-la-Trinité, in the central valley of the Monterosa area.

Innichen
Valley town in Pustertal on northern side of the Dolomites, with a small area of slopes but also close to the more extensive linked area of 3 Zinnen. San Candido is the Italian name.

Isolaccia – Alta Valtellina – 16
Valley village at base of gondola into small Cima Piazzi ski area, near Bormio.

Jouvenceaux – Via Lattea – 136
Almost a suburb of Sauze d'Oulx.

Kronplatz – 61

Latemar, Ski Center – Southern Dolomites – 126
Name now attached to a small ski area off Val di Fassa linking Predazzo to Obereggen.

Limone Piemonte
Fair-sized resort in the maritime Alps south of Turin, at one end of worthwhile Riserva Bianca ski area.

Livigno – Alta Valtellina – 16

Macugnaga
A pair of quiet, pretty villages dramatically set at the head of a remote valley, over the mountains from Zermatt and Saas-Fee. It's a place for a cheap holiday away from it all, with some skiing thrown in.

Madesimo – 67

Madonna di Campiglio – 72

Malcesine
Large summer resort on Lake Garda with a small area of slopes on Monte Baldo, accesed by a revolving cable car. Spectacular views over the lake.

Malga Ciapela – Sella Ronda – 99
Minor resort at the foot of the Marmolada glacier massif, with a link into the Sella Ronda via Arabba.

Marilleva – Madonna di Campiglio – 72
Small modern ski station linked to Madonna di Campiglio's extensive intermediate slopes.

Moena – Southern Dolomites – 126
Lovely old down in lower Val di Fassa with varied skiing nearby on Alpe Lusia.

Mondolè Ski
Fair sized area in the maritime Alps south of Turin, shared by Frabosa Soprana, Prato Nevoso and Artesina.

Monte Bondone
Trento's local hill, only a few minutes' drive away from the town. For a local hill it is excellent and the whole of the small area is covered by snowmaking. Great views to the Brenta Dolomites around Madonna.
Monterosa – 81
Nova Levante – Southern Dolomites – 126
Village close to Bozen/Bolzano at one end of Carezza ski area extending to Passo Costalunga.
Obereggen – Southern Dolomites – 126
Tiny resort close to Bozen/ Bolzano at one end of Latemar slopes also accessible from Predazzo in Val di Fiemme.
Olang – Kronplatz – 61
Minor base for Kronplatz, not far from Bruneck. Italian name is Valdaora.
Ortisei – Sella Ronda – 99
Charming, lively, old market town in Val Gardena, down the valley from Selva and the Sella Ronda.
Pampeago – Southern Dolomites – 126
Tiny ski station in the centre of the Latemar area shared with Predazzo and Obereggen.
Passo Costalunga – Sella Ronda – 99
Cluster of lodgings on a low pass, close to Val di Fassa, at one end of Carezza area extendng to Nova Levante.
Passo Rolle – Southern Dolomites – 126
Small group of lifts either side of the road over a high pass just north of San Martino di Castrozza.
Passo San Pellegrino – Southern Dolomites – 126
Smallish ski area south of the Sella Ronda, with lifts each side of the pass road and links with the valley village of Falcade.
Passo dello Stelvio
Summer skiing area near Bormio, set on the second-highest road pass in the Alps (2758m).
Passo Tonale – Ponte di Legno-Tonale – 93
Main resort of the rebranded Ponte di Legno-Tonale ski area.
Pejo
Small resort with high skiing off Val di Sole, between Passo Tonale and Madonna di Campiglio.
Pila – 88
Pinzolo – Madonna di Campiglio – 72
Valley village with wooded slopes linked to Madonna di Campiglio.
Plan de Corones – 61
Italian name for Kronplatz.
Plose
One of two worthwhile little areas within reach of Brixen/Bressanone (the other being Gitschberg).

Ponte di Legno – 93
Attractive sheltered alternative to Passo Tonale, with which it shares its slopes.
Pozza di Fassa – Sella Ronda – 99
Small village in Val di Fassa, sharing an area of slopes with Alba, and thus linked to the Sella Ronda.
Pragelato – Via Lattea – 136
Inexpensive base, linked by cable car to Sestriere.
Prato Nevoso
Purpose-built resort, part of Mondolè ski area south of Turin shared with Artesina and Frabosa Soprana.
Predazzo – Southern Dolomites – 126
Small, quiet place in Val di Fiemme, at one end of Latemar area extending via Pampeago to Obereggen.
Reischach – Kronplatz – 61
Bruneck's lift base for Kronplatz. Italian name is Riscone.
Riscone – Kronplatz – 61
Italian name for Reischach.
San Candido
Valley town in Val Pusteria on northern side of the Dolomites, with a small area of slopes but also close to the more extensive linked area of 3 Zinnen. Innichen is its German name.
San Cassiano – Sella Ronda – 99
A quiet, pretty village with some good hotels, sharing an extensive area of easy skiing with Corvara, on the Sella Ronda circuit.
San Martino di Castrozza – Southern Dolomites – 126
Pleasant village in a spectacular Dolomite setting, with modest area of slopes (and more up the road at Passo Rolle).
Sansicario – Via Lattea – 136
Tiny, modern resort, well placed near Sauze d'Oulx in the Via Lattea.
Santa Caterina – Alta Valtellina – 16
Quiet village with its own small ski area, a bus-ride east of Bormio.
Santa Cristina – Sella Ronda – 99
Quiet village in Val Gardena, linked in to the Sella Ronda circuit.
Santa Fosca – Southern Dolomites – 126
One of several small resort villages sharing the fairly extensive Civetta ski area.
San Vigilio di Marebbe – Kronplatz – 61
Main destination resort for Kronplatz.
Sauze d'Oulx – Via Lattea – 136
Schnalstal
High area in the Dolomites near Merano with slopes reaching glacial heights and a top-of-the-mountain hotel that is the highest in the Alps. Val Senales is its Italian name.

Schöneben
Small ski area close to Austrian border, shared by St Valentin and Reschen.
Seiseralm – Sella Ronda – 99
German name of Alpe di Siusi, an extensive slope area above Ortisei in Val Gardena.
Sella Nevea
Limited but developing resort in a beautiful setting on the Slovenian border, and now linked to Bovec-Kanin.
Sella Ronda – 99
Selva / Val Gardena – Sella Ronda – 99
The biggest resort on the Sella Ronda circuit.
Sesto
Italian name for Sexten.
Sestriere – Via Lattea – 136
Sexten
Small village off the Pusteral on the north side of the Dolomites, sharing the fair-sized 3 Zinnen area with Vierschach. Sesto is its Italian name.
Siusi – Sella Ronda – 99
Valley town with a long, powerful gondola up to the Alpe di Siusi area above Ortisei. Seis is the German name.
Solda
Italian name for Sulden.
Stafal – Monterosa – 81
Central lift base of the Monterosa area, at the head of the Gressoney valley.
St Vigil in Enneberg – Kronplatz – 61
German name for San Vigilio – main destination resort for Kronplatz.
Sulden
Remote village over the Stelvio pass from Bormio, with lifts on three mountains, one of them reaching glacial heights. Solda is its German name.
Temù – Ponte di Legno-Tonale – 93
Hamlet down the valley from Ponte di Legno, with a lift into the skiing.
La Thuile – Espace San Bernardo – 54
Italian resort sharing Espace San Bernardo with French La Rosière.
Valdaora – Kronplatz – 61
Minor base for Kronplatz, not far from Bruneck. German name is Olang.
Val di Fassa – Sella Ronda – 99
Valley containing Campitello and Canazei – part of the Sella Ronda circuit.
Val di Fiemme – Southern Dolomites – 126
Valley below Val di Fassa; name is often used in association with Latemar ski area above Predazzo.
Val di Zoldo – Southern Dolomites – 126
Valley containing several small resort villages sharing the fairly extensive Civetta ski area.

Val Gardena – Sella Ronda – 99
Valley area containing Selva, Ortisei and Santa Cristina – linked to the Sella Ronda circuit.
Valgrisenche
Small, peaceful village on the southern side of the Aosta valley. Established heli-ski centre – about 20 drop points on the local peaks. A couple of intermediate runs, nursery area and a few cross-country loops.
Val Senales
High area in the Dolomites near Merano with slopes reaching glacial heights and a top-of-the-mountain hotel that is the highest in the Alps. Schnalstal is its German name.
Valtournenche – Cervinia – 33
Cheaper, lower back-door point of entry to Cervinia slopes.
Versciaco
Small village off the Alta Val Pusteria on the north side of the Dolomites, sharing the fair-sized 3 Zinnen area with Sesto. Vierschach is its German name.
Vierschach
Italian name for Versciaco.
Vigo di Fassa – Sella Ronda – 99
Neat village in Val di Fassa, with a cable car into the small but scenic Catinaccio area of slopes.
La Villa – Sella Ronda – 99
Village sharing with Corvara and San Cassiano an area of mainly easy skiing just off the Sella Ronda circuit.

For your notes
If they're observations on a ski resort, please share them with us: reports@wheretoski.co.uk